The Narrative of Cabeza de Vaca

The Narrative of Cabeza de Vaca

Álvar Núñez Cabeza de Vaca

Edited, translated, and
with an introduction
by Rolena Adorno and
Patrick Charles Pautz

UNIVERSITY OF NEBRASKA PRESS : LINCOLN & LONDON

LIBRARY OF CONGRESS CATALOGING-IN-PUBLICATION DATA
Núñez Cabeza de Vaca, Álvar, 16th cent.
[Relación y comentarios. English]
The narrative of Cabeza de Vaca / Álvar Núñez Cabeza de Vaca ; edited, translated, and with an introduction by Rolena Adorno and Patrick Charles Pautz.
p. cm. Includes bibliographical references (p.) and index.
ISBN 0-8032-1528-2 (cloth: alk. paper) – ISBN 0-8032-6416-x (pbk: alk. paper).
1. Núñez Cabeza de Vaca, Álvar, 16th cent. 2. Explorers – America – Biogra-
phy. 3. Explorers – Spain – Biography. 4. America – Discovery and explora-
tion – Spanish. 5. America – Early accounts to 1600. 6. Indians of North
America – Southwestern States. I. Adorno, Rolena. II. Pautz, Patrick Charles.
III. Title.
E125.N9 A3 2003 970.01'6'092–dc21 [B] 2002028986

CONTENTS

ILLUSTRATIONS

The Narrative of Cabeza de Vaca

When Thomas Jefferson remarked in a letter to a friend in 1787 that citizens of the new United States should study the Spanish language, he gave as one of the reasons the fact that "the ancient part of American history is written chiefly in Spanish" (Jefferson 11:558). Jefferson had in mind the accounts of the earliest European exploration, conquest, and settlement in the Americas that are found in narrative texts that extend from Columbus's letters from the Antilles through the reports, chronicles, and histories of the conquests of Mexico and Peru. His notion of American history was a hemispheric one, one which embraced the Circum-Caribbean area and North and South America, and the authors of that early history were Spanish. Most of those firsthand accounts of the cycles of European and Amerindian contact, as well as the great synthetic histories of Spain's intervention in the Americas, narrated the Spanish wars of conquest in which the European triumphed over the Amerindian. The firsthand reporters and learned historians wrote about Amerindian cultures and customs only secondarily.

Within this larger context of Spanish New World writings, Álvar Núñez Cabeza de Vaca's 1542 *Relación* is unique as the tale of the first Europeans and the first African to confront and survive the peopled wilderness of North America. Among captivity narratives Cabeza de Vaca's account tells a unique story of survival against the highest odds. It offers the repeated spectacle of first encounters between inhabitants of the Old World and those of New World lands unknown to them, and it foregrounds native Amerindian peoples, their customs, and their interactions with the newcomers in a manner seldom seen in expeditionary writings. The work fires the reader's imagination as it simultaneously documents historical occurrences of the actual Spanish expedition and describes the peoples, flora, and fauna of pre-Columbian North America. For these reasons contemporary history, ethnohistory, and archaeology have examined it for fresh clues about the North American past, contemporary fiction and film have recreated its timeless characters and plot, and current literary and cultural readings strive to suggest its myriad and ultimate meanings.

Cabeza de Vaca's vivid account offers the earliest European depiction of the vast expanse of continental North America. The events narrated by

Cabeza de Vaca occurred not long after the conquest of Mexico. The year was 1527: Juan Ponce de León and other Spanish explorers and conquerors had already chanced upon the Florida Peninsula in their search for gold and slaves, but it would be nearly a century later that the English would found Jamestown (1607) and land at Plymouth Rock (1620). Cabeza de Vaca and three other expeditionary survivors thus experienced areas of the future United States as no natives of Europe or Africa previously had done. They explored the lands of the Florida Peninsula, coasted the northern shore of the Gulf of Mexico on rafts, lived for six and a half years among the native groups of eastern coastal Texas, traversed northern Mexico and southwestern Texas on foot, and ultimately encountered their countrymen in Spanish Nueva Galicia in northwestern Mexico before proceeding on to the ancient city of México-Tenochtitlán, the capital of New Spain (see map 1).

Cabeza de Vaca's account starts as a typical conquest narrative. He tells how the Pánfilo de Narváez expedition, on which he served as one of the king's treasury officials, gathered supplies in the Caribbean for war and settlement on the mainland in *Florida* (the area named in Narváez's grant that consisted of the vast unexplored territories that lay beyond the northern frontier of New Spain from the Florida Peninsula to the unexplored Pacific Coast). Things went wrong, and it soon became a drama of survival without the force of arms amidst the variously hostile and friendly native groups of North America. The tables had turned: what had begun as the saga of some six hundred men (and ten women) bound for conquest and settlement along the northern rim of the Gulf of Mexico became the fascinating tale of four men, told from the perspective of one of them, living separated and in captivity before being reunited and beginning, nearly a year after that, their dramatic journey of escape.

The Cabeza de Vaca account brings us the Atlantic world not only along its Spain–North America axis but also along that of Portugal in relation to Africa and India. The Portugal–West Africa nexus is epitomized in the figure of Estevanico, the black Arabic-speaking African slave from Portuguese-held Azemmour in coastal northwestern Africa, one of the four survivors of the overland North American trek. Cabeza de Vaca's journey home opens out on to the horizons of the sixteenth-century Iberian world: the Spanish treasure ship on which he traveled was accosted by French privateers in the Azores and saved by a nine-ship Portuguese armada that included in its convoy several vessels returning to Europe from Africa and India. One was a slave ship inbound from West Africa; three others came from India bearing the magnificent, fragrant bounty of the Portuguese spice trade. In short, the Atlantic and global perspectives of his times are explicit in Cabeza de Vaca's *relación*.

The Mediterranean and Atlantic Worlds of Cabeza de Vaca

Álvar Núñez Cabeza de Vaca's personal experience (1485–92 to ca. 1559) and ancestral lineage offer similarly broad perspectives, reminding us that life in provincial Andalusia for a man of military tradition and vocation was likely to be anything but confined to local affairs. At the end of his account he lauded his paternal grandfather, Pedro de Vera Mendoza, by identifying him as the conqueror of the island of Gran Canaria in the Canary Islands. His maternal lineage, whose name of Cabeza de Vaca he bore, dated back at least as far as the early thirteenth century. *Caballeros,* or members of the untitled middle-ranking nobility, of the Cabeza de Vaca line had participated in the "reconquest" of Spain from the Muslims. Fernán Ruiz Cabeza de Vaca's chronicled participation in the Christian conquest of Córdoba in 1236, which took place under the leadership of one of the most celebrated Christian monarchs of medieval Spain—Fernando III of Castile and León—links the Cabeza de Vaca name with one of the major military offensives of its era. (The popular legend that the Cabeza de Vaca name was created when bestowed on a humble shepherd for his role in the battle of Las Navas de Tolosa in 1212 is apocryphal.) (See Adorno and Pautz 1:298–308.)

Cabeza de Vaca's life story is cartographically projected onto the map that traces his journeys in Europe and to the Americas (see map 2). Like many Andalusians of his regional and familial traditions and other men of his generation, this native of Jerez de la Frontera was oriented first to the Mediterranean and then, fully, to the Atlantic. While his forebears had occupied themselves on the frontiers of Muslim Spain in Andalusia and on the seacoasts of southern Spain and northern Africa, Cabeza de Vaca and his contemporaries were involved in even broader international domains. National and international conflicts during the reigns of King Ferdinand of Aragon and his grandson, King Charles I of Spain, were part of Cabeza de Vaca's military experience before he set sail, for the first time, to the Indies.

Serving the house of the dukes of Medina Sidonia from his youth until his departure for America (1503–27), Cabeza de Vaca's career at arms spanned the period of King Ferdinand's North African campaigns and the defense and expansion of his Aragonese territories in Italy (1511–13). In Italy, under Ferdinand's banner, Cabeza de Vaca participated in the 1512 battles of Ravenna and Bologna and the siege of the lands of the duke of Ferrara. As a reward he was appointed royal standard bearer (*alférez*) of the city of Gaeta, near Naples (see map 2, and Adorno and Pautz 1:350–66). The *relación* (f42v) contains an occasional, fleeting reference to these earlier military experiences. When Cabeza de Vaca recalled the warlike character of the natives of eastern coastal Texas, he remarked, "they have as much cunning to protect themselves from their enemies as they would have if they had been raised in Italy and in continuous war."

In 1520–21 Cabeza de Vaca again supported the crown while in the employ of the dukes of Medina Sidonia during the early years of the reign of Charles I of Spain (Charles V of the Holy Roman Empire). In Spain in 1521 Cabeza de Vaca participated in the final defeat of the year-long Comunero uprising that threatened the stability of the Castilian state by reasserting local needs and interests against Charles's new centralized royal power and the threat of his treasury-draining wars abroad. In the same year Cabeza de Vaca participated in the battle of Puente de la Reina, in Navarre, in which Charles's forces repelled those of Francis I of France in the first of the series of wars between those monarchs (see Adorno and Pautz 1:366–69).

Cabeza de Vaca's easy familiarity with European and Mediterranean reference points reveals the breadth of his personal horizons as a military man and as a mariner. His Indies career was remarkable for its geographical range over North and South America, first to *Florida* as royal treasurer and later to Río de la Plata as governor of the province centered at Asunción, in today's Paraguay (see map 2). His governorship lasted from March 1541 until April 1544, when he was arrested and imprisoned for eleven months before being sent home in chains, arriving back in Spain in September 1545. He was tried by the Royal Council of the Indies on criminal charges that included misconduct in office, mistreating the Indians, and raising his own heraldic standard when he should have raised the king's. In 1551 he was found guilty and sentenced to be stripped of all titles conferred on him, banned in perpetuity from the Indies, and banished to the penal colony of Oran on the North African coast for five years of service to the emperor at his own expense. Cabeza de Vaca appealed the sentence, and in 1552 it was reduced: his banishment from the Indies henceforth pertained only to Río de la Plata, and he was relieved from the obligation of five years of service in Oran. The perpetual loss of his titles was still apparently in effect, as was his liability for court costs and any civil suits that might be brought against him. Nevertheless, the royal license to print the 1555 edition of his work, which was signed by the Infanta Juana on behalf of her brother, Prince Philip (the future Philip II), identified Cabeza de Vaca by his Río de la Plata title of governor. Ironically, by apparent bureaucratic error the phrase "el governador Álvar Núñez Cabeza de Vaca" in the royal license mistakenly referred to the Narváez expedition to North America (see Adorno and Pautz 1:283, 382–402).

Even in his last days, when back home in Jerez de la Frontera, Andalusia, Cabeza de Vaca looked outward: the last known, documented public act of his life was his 1559 ransom of a distant relative, Hernán Ruiz Cabeza de Vaca, who was being held captive by the king of Algiers after being captured in an expedition against the Ottoman Turk. As a member of the *caballero* class of the Jerez de la Frontera house of Cabeza de Vaca, our Álvar Núñez (often synonymously referred to as an "hidalgo") almost certainly ended his days in Jerez de la Frontera, and is probably interred in the Dominican convent of Santo Domingo el Real where his paternal grandfather, Pedro de Vera Mendoza, had been buried. (The popular notion that Cabeza de Vaca died "penniless, old, and broken-hearted" in Valladolid is another bit of oft-repeated but unsubstantiated apocrypha. See Adorno and Pautz 1:407–12.) For the fates of the three other overland survivors of the Narváez expedition see Adorno and Pautz 2:407–28.

The Geography of the *Relación* and Consideration of the Route

Charles V and, by extension, his ministers who oversaw the affairs of the Indies, were the original intended readers of Cabeza de Vaca's *relación* (see the later section entitled "Writing the *Relación* to the Emperor"). By the time a version of Cabeza de Vaca's account reached them in 1537, Spanish officials had spent almost half a century watching the Spanish American empire unfold from its center in the Caribbean. These men were intimately familiar with the physical and political geography of the Americas, and Cabeza de Vaca's geographical references in the *relación* appropriately assume that knowledge. Cabeza de Vaca's account represented a fundamental contribution to this continuously evolving corpus of information, even as he sought to influence its development through his own report. From a remove of almost five hundred years, a modern-day comprehension of Cabeza de Vaca's account naturally requires the definition of geographical terminology and identification of geographical locators whose significance was obvious to its intended readers in the 1530s and 1540s.

Spanish exploration of the southern Gulf of Mexico originated from Cuba and followed along the Gulf's southern rim, from the tip of the Yucatán Peninsula to the region of modern-day Cabo Rojo (north of Veracruz) between 1517 and 1519. This exploration led ultimately to Cortés's discovery and conquest of Tenochtitlán, and in the ensuing years he expanded his control over central Mexico, which came to be known as New Spain, in all directions. One outcome of this expansion was the conquest of Pánuco and the establishment in 1523 of Santisteban del Puerto near the mouth of the Río Pánuco in present-day central Tamaulipas, Mexico (see map 1). Cortés's impulse for founding this settlement was to push the frontier of his conquests as far north and east along the coast as possible in response to competing exploration moving west along the northern coast of the Gulf of Mexico at that time.

This westward-moving exploration of the northern coast of the Gulf of Mexico had its precursor in Juan Ponce de León's discovery of the Florida Peninsula in 1513. Apparently incited by the promising discoveries along the southern coast of the Gulf of Mexico, Francisco de Garay, the governor of the island of Jamaica (known then as Santiago), sent exploratory expeditions from Jamaica along the entire expanse of the northern Gulf Coast in 1518 and 1519. In the summer of 1519 Garay's men confronted Cortés's men briefly at a location north of Cabo Rojo on the western Gulf Coast. Garay's subsequent activities in the region along the northern Gulf of Mexico did not receive the detailed historical treatment that Cortés's conquests in New Spain did, largely because the attempts failed miserably. Nevertheless, primary sources and all of the early histories point to Garay's attempt to establish a settlement on the northwestern Gulf Coast, most likely at the mouth of the Río Pánuco, during the summer of 1519 or earlier (see Adorno and Pautz 3:227–45).

Garay launched a final failed attempt to found a settlement at Pánuco in the summer of 1523, only to find upon his arrival that Cortés had already founded Santisteban del Puerto there. Cortés's officials at Santisteban del Puerto suggested to Garay that he take his men back to either the Río de las Palmas or the Río del Espíritu Santo to found a settlement. Both rivers were known to be in the direction of the Florida Peninsula with respect to Santisteban del Puerto; the mouth of the latter river was assumed to be approximately 200 leagues distant along the coast from the Spanish enclave. From 1523 onward Santisteban del Puerto, located slightly inland on the Río Pánuco, came to be known as the farthest northeastern outpost of Spanish settlement in New Spain along the coast of the Gulf of Mexico (see Adorno and Pautz 3:258–70).

By the time the Narváez expedition departed from Spain in 1527 it had been largely agreed that the Florida Peninsula was not an island, but rather a protrusion of a large northern land mass connected ultimately to the territories of New Spain. On 4 November 1525 Nuño Beltrán de Guzmán was named governor of the newly defined province of Pánuco, an area comprised of the northeastern territories conquered by Cortés with Santisteban del Puerto as its capital. The Spanish government separated Pánuco from New Spain in an attempt to limit Hernán Cortés's growing monopolistic influence on the mainland. Whereas the term *Florida* referred originally and specifically to the Florida Peninsula, by 1527 it had come to represent a legal jurisdiction representing the entire northern mass of land that extended from the tip of the peninsula to the vast territories north of the jurisdictions of New Spain and Pánuco. Knowing *Florida* to be attached to an ever-expanding landmass, Cabeza de Vaca likewise referred in the proem of his account (fiv) to the area as *tierra firme*, the mainland, distinguishing it from the Caribbean Islands.

When the Spanish monarch granted Pánfilo de Narváez his right to explore and conquer in this region on 11 December 1526, he specifically gave Narváez authority to "discover and conquer and settle the said territories that are from the Río de las Palmas to the cape of what is called *La Florida*" (Vas Mingo 234; see map 1). The concession makes reference to Narváez's earlier petition to explore and conquer *Florida* "from one sea to the other," with specific reference to the Río de las Palmas and the coastline between the mouth of that river and "the island of *La Florida*" (in other words, the Florida Peninsula). The two seas referenced were the North Sea, made up of the Atlantic Ocean and the Gulf of Mexico, and the South Sea, the Spaniards' name for the Pacific Ocean and Gulf of California. In Seville, on 30 August 1527 (only forty-five days after Narváez had set out from Sanlúcar de Barrameda for the Caribbean), a former Cortés expeditionary, Luis de Cárdenas, gave a formal opinion (*parecer*) regarding the jurisdictional divisions of New Spain (CDI 40:273–87). Cárdenas described the fourth section of New Spain as extending from the Río de las Palmas west to the opposite sea (the South Sea), and said that Pánfilo de Narváez was now going to conquer that region (CDI 40:280–81). Cárdenas believed that the distance from the Río de las Palmas west to the South Sea was 650 leagues and that from the river east to the Florida Peninsula was another 300. According to Cárdenas, not even three governors would be sufficient to bring under Spanish control the region that the crown had granted to Narváez.

The Río de las Palmas is today believed to be the Río Soto la Marina in the state of Tamaulipas in northeastern Mexico. As both the concession granted to Narváez and Luis de Cárdenas's testimony show, this river was the focal point for defining the province of *Florida* in 1527 and was the obvious intended destination of the Narváez expedition (see map 1). Once the Narváez expedition struck land on the Gulf Coast in April 1528, the motivation to identify a port at the mouth of a river along the coastline was driven initially by the intention of locating the Río de las Palmas in order to establish a settlement there. The frequent references to harboring the ships in a safe and populated port were clear references to the expedition's expectation of locating Santisteban del Puerto on the Río Pánuco nearby. The importance of these two rivers in Cabeza de Vaca's text gave rise to the directional references "the way of Palms" (*la vía de Palmas*) and "the way of Pánuco" (*la vía de Pánuco*), both of which signified travel along the coast in the direction of these rivers, and "the way of *Florida*" (*la vía de la Florida*), which signified travel along the coast toward the Florida Peninsula. Over time Cabeza de Vaca came to refer to travel toward the Río de las Palmas and the Río Pánuco as traveling ahead (*adelante*) and to locations in the opposite direction as behind or back (*atrás*).

In light of the Narváez expedition's geographic knowledge and the obvious intended destination of the Río de las Palmas to the north of Santisteban del Puerto on the west side of the Gulf of Mexico, the expedition's actual landfall on the east side of the Gulf of Mexico, on the west coast of the Florida Peninsula, is disorienting, and it persists as one of two geographical conundrums regarding the Narváez expedition and Cabeza de Vaca's account. In his *relación* Cabeza de Vaca never explicitly states the expedition's intended destination nor does he explicitly address the magnitude of the error at any time. The spectacular outcome of the expedition made it impossible to conceal the fact that the expedition did not reach its intended destination. Yet in his writing Cabeza de Vaca never confronts the issue directly. Instead, at the end of his text, in a most matter-of-fact way, he observes that the bay the Narváez expedition discovered lies 100 leagues north of the port of Havana. The subtlety of the comment and the silence on the scope of the expedition's error are such that some readers come away from the text with the false understanding that the west coast of the Florida Peninsula was the expedition's originally intended destination, and that the Narváez men were simply unable to locate a known port on that coast which Spaniards such as Ponce de León and the men of Francisco de Garay's expedition had previously visited.

In his account Cabeza de Vaca repeats over and over the expeditionaries' goal of reaching Pánuco, and it appears to have persisted as the objective of the final four survivors, at least through the summer of 1535. The importance of reaching the river and the Spanish settlement of Santisteban del Puerto has significant implications regarding Cabeza de Vaca's silence on the second unanswered geography question of the *relación*—the four survivors' ultimate abandonment of their coastal search for Santisteban del Puerto and their unexpected crossing of the entire expanse of northern Mexico to reach the Gulf of California and the Pacific Ocean. When we consider the state of Spanish exploration of the Pacific coast and of western New Spain prior to 1528 when the Narváez expeditionaries entered *Florida*, the fact that the Narváez expedition survivors ended up following the path they did takes on an even more astounding dimension.

Vasco Núñez de Balboa's discovery of the Pacific Ocean (known to the Spaniards as the South Sea) in 1513 was preceded by nearly a decade of speculation about the existence of a southern sea that would offer great wealth through direct access to Cathay and Great India. On 16 September 1522 Sebastián del Cano, Magellan's Spanish navigator, arrived in Spain following his circumnavigation of the globe, and the existence of the vast Pacific Ocean became widely known. Certainly most directly influential on the Narváez expedition survivors, however, would have been the publication in 1523 and 1525 of Cortés's third and fourth letters of relation (see Adorno and Pautz 3:291–306). In the third letter of relation, dated 15 May 1522, Cortés announced his men's arrival at the South Sea from México-Tenochtitlán. The title page to the published edition of this letter announced how Cortés "relates how he discovered the South Sea and many more great provinces, very rich in gold and pearls and precious stones; and how he has even heard tell that there are spices" (Pagden 160; Cortés, *Cartas de relación* 310). In his third letter Cortés placed the South Sea at twelve to fourteen days' journey from México-Tenochtitlán, and spoke of plans to construct ships for the purpose of exploration in the South Sea and along the coast (Adorno and Pautz 3:299). Whereas Cortés's third letter of relation spoke of riches in connection with New Spain's potential proximity to Asia, Cortés's fourth letter of relation, dated 15 October 1524, was the source of considerable expectations about the wealth of the South Sea in its own right. Specifically, Cortés detailed in his fourth letter that his men had traveled from Zacatula to Colima, where they had founded a settlement, and that pearls and a good harbor had been discovered there (Adorno and Pautz 3:302).

Cortés's letters alone suffice to explain the expectations the Narváez expeditionaries would have had about the wealth of the South Sea; the constant undercurrent and frequent direct references in Cabeza de Vaca's account to the possibility of discovering great wealth along the whole course of the Narváez expedition were undoubtedly inspired by Cortés's discovery and conquest of México-Tenochtitlán. The information emanating from Cortés's conquests likewise may have been the source of the Narváez expeditionaries' significantly understated notion of the distance to be traveled in crossing New Spain if they equated it with the well-known route between Veracruz and México-Tenochtitlán plus some additional fourteen days to travel from México-Tenochtitlán to the coast of the South Sea. In contrast to their thinking, however, stands Luis de Cárdenas's testimony from 1527 (mentioned earlier) that the distance from the Río de las Palmas to the South Sea was 650 leagues (nearly two thousand miles). Whatever the Narváez expeditionaries' expectations about this distance were, those expectations would have been a direct influence on the men's decision to follow the overland course.

The most perplexing aspect of the Narváez expeditionaries' crossing of northern Mexico and southwestern Texas between late summer 1535 and April 1536 is the complete absence in Cabeza de Vaca's account of any explicit reference to the great risk the men took in abandoning their much more certain coastal search for Santisteban del Puerto on the Río Pánuco in exchange for the unknown overland route. Cabeza de Vaca (f49v, f54r–v) acknowledges the men's motivation—the discovery of material wealth—for seeking the South Sea; he does not acknowledge directly, however, that they set out across lands whose extent and harshness were completely unknown to his countrymen at the time.

The absence of a clear declaration and turning point in the narrative was a strong influence on modern readers' hypotheses about the route that the men followed, with the general effect being an assumed abandonment by the men of their coastal route at a point much earlier in the account than the narrative's contents can support. It is important to note that the statement Cabeza de Vaca made in the *relación* just after he narrated the men's sighting of mountains near the North Sea (Gulf of Mexico) for the first time on their journey along the coast, can easily be misinterpreted as an explicit declaration of the men's intention to leave their coastal route and cross over to the Pacific coast:

> All the people of the coast are very bad, and we considered it preferable to go through the land because the people farther inland are of a better disposition and they treated us better, and we considered it certain that we would find the land more populated and with better means of sustenance. Finally, we did this because, by crossing through the land, we would see many of its particularities, because if God our Lord were served by taking some one of us out of there and bringing him to the land of Christians, he could give an account and description of it. (f47v)

While this passage might seem to convey explicitly the men's resolution to cross overland to the Pacific, in fact it says only that the Narváez survivors elected to follow along the coast but through the interior rather than directly along the coastline (see Adorno and Pautz 2:169–78). The strand of interpretation that identifies the mountains that the men sighted at this juncture as being located in western Texas (thinking which therefore questions the accuracy or interpretation of Cabeza de Vaca's reference to the North Sea with regard to these mountains), dates back as far as Buckingham Smith (1851) and continues to be repeated by modern editors and translators. We identify these mountains as the Sierra de Pamoranes near the Gulf Coast between the mouths of the Rio Grande to the north and the Río Conchos–San Fernando to the south (see map 1, and Adorno and Pautz 2:170–72).

As one of the keenest early readers of Cabeza de Vaca's account, Las Casas (*Apologética* 2:361 [chap. 206]) understood the coastal nature of the majority of the Narváez expeditionaries' travels and the subtle difference between the exploration of coastline versus coastal inlands that the men carried out on the Texas-Mexico coast prior to ultimately crossing over from the North Sea to the South Sea: "[f]inally, all these peoples, or the majority of those which Cabeza de Vaca saw and with whom he had contact, and of whom he relates the said customs are the ones near the coast of the North Sea, and those who neighbor them, and not very many leagues inland, since afterward he strayed far from the sea, entering into the land and encountering many other diverse and more organized nations, about whose customs he could learn very little, as he was traveling very rapidly." Writing in the 1550s, Las Casas did not comment on the geographical perplexities of the Cabeza de Vaca account. He neither marveled at how far from their intended destination the Narváez expeditionaries had landed, nor commented on the incredible distance through completely uncharted lands that the four Narváez expedition survivors had almost miraculously traveled. Perhaps in an era of radically changing geographic perceptions, events such as those that Cabeza de Vaca experienced seemed far more comprehensible and far less remarkable than they do today. In contrast to this notion, however, stands Cabeza de Vaca's own comment in the proem to the 1555 edition on the delights of contemplating the twists of fate he had experienced (see later section entitled "Destined for a Broader Readership").

The closest Cabeza de Vaca ever comes to commenting directly on his overland journey's scope is to say that he understood that "from one coast to the other at its widest point, the distance may be two hundred leagues" (f63r). He is silent on the fact that he and the other three survivors of the Narváez expedition apparently narrowly missed their goal of reaching Santisteban del Puerto as they traveled along the coast before embarking in the summer of 1535 on their trek across northern Mexico. Had they traveled south along the western coast of the Gulf of Mexico even as far as the Río de las Palmas they might have discovered remnants there of Nuño de Guzmán's 1527 explorations to that river. Likewise, Cabeza de Vaca does not observe the fact that it was sheer luck on the survivors' part that by the time they reached the area that is today the southern portion of the Mexican state of Sonora in the spring of 1536, they found Spaniards there; Nuño de Guzmán had extended the frontier of New Spain (as Cabeza de Vaca would have known it in 1528) northward along the coast of the South Sea all the way to the Río Yaqui between 1531 and 1533, naming the newly organized province Nueva Galicia (see map 1, and Adorno and Pautz 3:352–75). Upon reentry into the sphere of Spanish-dominated lands, the surviving Narváez expeditionaries must have undergone substantial debriefing, in which they would have opened their countrymen's eyes onto the vast territories of North America to the north of New Spain. Likewise, their compatriots would have related to them the monumental developments of Spanish exploration in the Americas that they had missed in their absence between 1528 and 1536. Among the most spectacular of these was the Spanish search for, and invasion of, the Inca empire in Peru in 1530–32.

Temporal Flow and Narrative Complexity of the *Relación*

From a narrative perspective Cabeza de Vaca's *relación* initially appears to be a simple, straightforward, linear account of the Narváez expedition. Beginning with the narration of the Narváez expedition's departure from Spain in June 1527, all the way through to the description of the end of the overwintering on the island of Malhado in Galveston Bay by the expeditionaries of Cabeza de Vaca's and Alonso del Castillo and Andrés Dorantes's rafts in the spring of 1529, the narrative represents a single strand. Time and space travel forward together over the course of almost the first half of the account (f3r–f27r). The narrative carries the expedition from Spain to the Caribbean to the Florida Peninsula, and along the northern Gulf Coast to the Texas coast, and recounts the passage of time from June 1527 through April 1529.

Commencing with Cabeza de Vaca's account of his own time on the Texas coast after nearly all of the other expeditionaries had departed from the region in April 1529, the narrative structure of the *relación* maintains its linearity in the strictest sense as it continues to rigorously follow Cabeza de Vaca's personal trajectory. Nevertheless, it undergoes a dramatic transformation not only in that the underlying linear structure is suddenly forced to bear an immense amount of descriptive material pertaining to observations Cabeza de Vaca made largely while living on the Texas coast, but also in that it continually bifurcates as Cabeza de Vaca narrates the information he gained from his fellow expeditionaries upon being reunited with them.

Even prior to describing his reunion with Andrés Dorantes, Alonso del Castillo, and Estevanico, Cabeza de Vaca's account undergoes a temporal shift. While the narrative displays a relatively rapid passage of space and time up to the men's arrival and overwintering at Malhado through April 1529, the narration of the ensuing four years, through the early summer of 1533, is marked by a virtual standstill. Cabeza de Vaca alludes both to his movements forward from Malhado many leagues down the coast in the direction of Pánuco and to his return trips along the same course back to Malhado. Without question it was this lengthy stationary period that Cabeza de Vaca spent among the native peoples of the Galveston Bay area that allowed him to collect a significant portion of the information that he provides in the *relación*.

Cabeza de Vaca's reunion with the other expeditionaries in the spring of 1533 also necessitated the "turning back of time" in the narrative. His account becomes an account within an account within an account, as he conveys the following narratives: (1) Andrés Dorantes, Alonso del Castillo and Estevanico's travel down the coast with eleven other men in the spring of 1529, until their encounter that same spring-summer with Figueroa; (2) Figueroa's account to Dorantes, Castillo, and Estevanico of his experience from the time of his departure from Malhado in November 1528 with Méndez and two others, who went from Malhado in search of Pánuco until he encountered Esquivel, perhaps in the spring of 1529; and (3) Esquivel's account to Figueroa of the arrival in the autumn of 1528 on the Texas coast of the raft on which he had traveled and the one of Narváez, and the demise of all these men by the spring of 1529 until Esquivel encountered Figueroa. As each of these subsequent narratives was interrupted by its intersection with the next, Cabeza de Vaca was left with the task of verbally retracing his steps and narrating the remaining portion of the previously interrupted accounts. Unfortunately, he did not execute this portion of his narrative with the clarity he displayed in the narration of the initial portion of each narrative strand.

The account that remained to be told at the end of this series of interrupting stories concerned the fates of Figueroa and of the surviving members of the Dorantes-Castillo party of men whom he had joined in the spring-summer of 1529. Cabeza de Vaca successfully picked up the end of Figueroa's account, explicitly detailing how Figueroa told the Dorantes-Castillo party that Esquivel might still be in the region along the coast where they were located at the time. However, Cabeza de Vaca did not then mention the Dorantes-Castillo party's experience from 1529 through 1533 with a line such as, "And Dorantes and Castillo told me that after Figueroa conveyed all this information to them they . . ." as might have been expected. Instead, with the phrase "And as I have just said" ("Y como acabo de dezir," f31r), Cabeza de Vaca assumed the direct narration of what occurred among Dorantes, Castillo, Estevanico, Figueroa, and the other surviving men of the Dorantes-Castillo party as though he had witnessed it firsthand, even though he himself was separated from them during the entire four-year period, until 1533. Among the most significant events he narrates are Figueroa's flight down the coast with one of the other men (the Asturian) who had come with Dorantes and Castillo, the murder at the hands of the natives of three additional men who had come with Dorantes and Castillo (Diego Dorantes, Valdivieso, and Diego de Huelva), and Andrés Dorantes's movement to live among coastal inland-dwelling natives who, he learns, had killed Esquivel.

Prior to conveying all of these accounts, in narrating his own final movement down the Texas coast in the spring of 1533 Cabeza de Vaca gives an initial prefiguration of these events in the form of information he received from native people just prior to being reunited with Dorantes, Castillo, and Estevanico. Thus his reader learns that three men like him were alive somewhere ahead along the coast, that Diego Dorantes, Valdivieso, and Diego de Huelva had been killed, and that the natives who now held Andrés Dorantes (thus, implicitly identified as one of the "three men like him") had also killed Esquivel and Méndez. On a reader's first pass, however, this information is nearly unintelligible since the fates of all the groups who preceded Cabeza de Vaca down the coast four years earlier have not yet been revealed.

Cabeza de Vaca's account of Andrés Dorantes, Alonso del Castillo, and Estevanico's experience among the natives of the Texas coast between the spring of 1529 when they left Malhado and the spring of 1533 when Cabeza de Vaca was reunited with them (during which time he himself was living in the region of Galveston Bay), is commingled with lengthy descriptions of native customs and it is difficult to glean from his account a clear narrative of what occurred among these men during that time. Interestingly, in this regard Gonzalo Fernández de Oviedo y Valdés's account of the Narváez expedition, written from the Joint Report (see the section entitled "Oviedo's and Santa Cruz's Histories of the Narváez Expedition"), offers an independent, parallel account that is clearly drawn from Andrés Dorantes's own testimony regarding this period and offers a substantial, fully corroborative supplement to Cabeza de Vaca's *relación* (Oviedo 3:593a–95a, 598b–601b). The most provocative detail from the Oviedo material is the fact that Castillo, Dorantes, and Estevanico suffered a failed attempt to flee down the coast at the end of the summer in 1532, the year prior to being reunited with Cabeza de Vaca. The very survival of Cabeza de Vaca and the existence of the *relación* as we know it can be attributed to that failure.

In subsequent narration Cabeza de Vaca delivers nearly perfect closure on the fates of all the Narváez expeditionaries. This act of narrative completion comes always in the form of tangible eyewitness testimony: (1) Andrés Dorantes confirms the death of Esquivel among the Mariames by discovering his personal effects among them; (2) Other natives farther down the coast give the four surviving Narváez expeditionaries an account of how the men of the Téllez-Peñalosa raft were killed; (3) The Avavares tell the men how Figueroa and the Asturian were with natives whom they called the "people of the figs"; and, finally, (4) Cabeza de Vaca closes his narrative with an account of what happened to the Narváez expedition's ships according to what he learned, he says, from people who had remained on the ships and to whom he later spoke in New Spain and in Castile nearly ten years after being separated from them on the west coast of the Florida Peninsula. There is no question that Cabeza de Vaca's narrative displays the characteristic long voyages and twists of fate typical of the Byzantine novel. Written retrospectively from Castile (as discussed below), the macrostructure of Cabeza de Vaca's *relación* is one of a series of interrupted accounts over a vast expanse of time and distance that reveals a final conclusion only as Cabeza de Vaca returns to his point of beginning.

Curiously, Cabeza de Vaca chose to place at the end of his account the prediction of the Muslim woman from Hornachos. Had he adhered rigorously to his technique of locating what we might call his "branch narrations" at the point in time when he received them in the "trunk narration" of his own trajectory, he most logically would have placed this episode at the point in his account just prior to relating his departure from the ships among some three hundred expeditionaries in April 1528 and their entrance into the Florida coastal interior. Whether or not Cabeza de Vaca consciously violated his own narrative protocol with regard to the placement of this item cannot be known. Nevertheless, it is interesting to consider the potential effect on the narrative of the alternative placement of the predicted failure of the Narváez expedition at the beginning of the account. Its presence at the end exercises a function of final closure, and some might question whether or not this occurrence was a literary embellishment. Without a doubt, Castilian superstition—here attributed to a Muslim woman and communicated through her Christian counterpart—was a reality of sixteenth-century Spain.

Certainly the narrative tension and ultimate completeness that the account exhibits explain some of its enduring textual vitality. Without seeking to disparage any literary pretensions Cabeza de Vaca might have had, it is probable that the major reason he selected his particular narrative structure was to document exactly whence he received all the information that he included in the *relación*. Ironically, it is the very completeness of Cabeza de Vaca's narrative, when read in isolation, that might lead a reader to question its veracity. Nevertheless, it was very likely that the confining nature of the geography of the Texas coastline ultimately enabled him to give such a complete account. Were it not for the sheer weight of the highly corroborative nature of the Oviedo text (particularly regarding Andrés Dorantes's testimony), as well as the bulk of external documentation that corroborates Cabeza de Vaca's own statements regarding the beginning and end of the expedition, one might reasonably question whether his account lies beyond the realm of history.

The methodical, linear quality that characterized the first portion of Cabeza de Vaca's narrative largely hangs in suspense until well after the remaining four Narváez expeditionaries set out on their final ten- to twelve-month journey from the Avavares Indians in late summer 1535. Though the account is unified into a single narration upon Cabeza de Vaca's reunion with the other three men in the spring of 1533, his narrative pertaining to this period (f31v–f45v) is heavily weighted with the description of native customs and characteristics that frequently cannot be assigned to a particular native group. Likewise, his narration of the men's experiences and interactions with the native peoples from the areas of Galveston Bay to extreme southern Texas are difficult to assign to particular moments in the period from the spring of 1533 to the late summer of 1535. In this portion of the account Cabeza de Vaca occasionally makes multiple isolated references to the passage of the same period of time or the same shift from one group of natives to another, only to abandon the reference immediately and return to additional descriptive narration. This tendency renders the tracking of the progression of time more difficult in this portion of the narrative.

Though reference to specific dates or even months almost disappears, Cabeza de Vaca's narration of the overland travel across northern Mexico and southwestern Texas regains its linear quality with regard to time and space and is easily followed until the men's reunion with Spaniards in northwestern Mexico in early 1536 (f45v–f59r). Cabeza de Vaca drafted the *relación* in Spain, sometime between 1538 and 1540, as evidenced by multiple references in the narrative to his presence there as he wrote. The methodical day-to-day references that characterize the early part of the account accustom the reader to associating its descriptive elements with their immediate space-time context. As days suddenly become years in the narrative and the steadily progressing linearity breaks down, it becomes more evident that Cabeza de Vaca wrote with his full nine-year experience continually in mind, and this important fact colors his entire account. A prime example of this retrospective dimension is the information Cabeza de Vaca conveyed about the American bison. While Cabeza de Vaca placed his description of the American bison at a point in his narrative that corresponds to a six-month period in 1533 while he was on the Texas coast, and during which time he and the other Narváez survivors waited to escape down the coast, his statement that the bison "extend over the land for more than four hundred leagues" (f34r) was almost certainly information that he did not receive until the men had reached a point much farther west on their overland journey to the South Sea (Pacific Ocean) between autumn 1535 and spring 1536.

The table that follows provides an analytical division of Cabeza de Vaca's *relación* into nine segments designed to facilitate the reader's access to the narrative, which is itself unbroken, and to call attention to the distinctiveness of its successive portions.

Analytical division of the *Relación*

Gulf Coast journey of the Narváez expedition (approx. 8 years):

Part	Period	Time	1542 folio	1555 chap.	Occurrences
1	17 June 1527 to Feb./Mar. 1528	8–9 mos.	f3r–f5v	1–2	Departure from Spain and sojourn in the Caribbean to arrival near Havana, Cuba
2	Feb./Mar. 1528 to 1 May 1528	2.5–3.5 mos.	f5v–f8v	3–4	Journey to *Florida* and establishment on the west coast of the Florida Peninsula
3 secs. 1–3	1 May 1528 to July 1536		f65v–f67r	38	Fate of the sea contingent and the search for Narváez's overland expedition
secs. 4–16	1 May 1528 to 22 Sept. 1528	5 mos.	f8v–f16r	5–8	Overland expedition into the Florida Peninsula to the Bay of Horses
4	22 Sept. 1528 to 6 Nov. 1528	1.5 mos.	f16r–f20v	9–10	Coastal exploration by raft to mouth of Mississippi River; separation of rafts and voyage to Texas coast
5	6 Nov. 1528 to midsummer 1535	81 mos. (6.5–6.75 yrs.)	f20v–f48r	11–28	Arrival of rafts at Galveston Bay; sojourn of expeditionaries among native peoples and travels south along the coast to the arrival of the final four survivors at the foot of mountains in northern Tamaulipas

Overland journey of the final four Narváez expedition survivors (approx. 2 years):

Part	Period	Time	1542 folio	1555 chap.	Occurrences
6	Midsummer 1535 to early autumn 1535	2–3 mos.	f48r–f54v	28–31	Four survivors' overland travel from northern Tamaulipas to La Junta de los Ríos
7	Early autumn 1535 to spring 1536	6–7 mos.	f54v–f58v	31–33	Four survivors' overland travel from La Junta de los Ríos to the Río Petatlán (Sinaloa)
8	Spring 1536 to 23 July 1536	3 mos.	f58v–f63v	33–36	Four survivors' reunion with other Spaniards and travel from the Río Petatlán to San Miguel de Culiacán and México-Tenochtitlán
9	23 July 1536 to 9 Aug. 1537	13 mos.	f63v–f65v	37	Four survivors' sojourn in México-Tenochtitlán and Cabeza de Vaca's travel to Havana, Cuba, and Lisbon, Portugal

Total: 122 mos. (10 yrs., 2 mos.)

Referentiality in the *Relación*, in the Sixteenth Century, and Today

When Cabeza de Vaca and his companions finally arrived in Nueva Galicia in 1536 they faced the enormous challenge of communicating to their countrymen in an intelligible way where they had been for the previous eight years, what had happened to them, and what was contained in the places they had lived in and traversed. Their task was made more difficult by the fact that they were uncertain about the location of the point along the coast of the Gulf of Mexico whence they had started, the extensive distance they had traveled, and the length of time they had been gone. In a sense, virtually everything was relative, and the circumstances of their experience placed them at great distance in space and time from any established point of reference. Yet in many regards the problem they faced was typical of expeditions of exploration and conquest of the day.

Without a doubt, the biggest question was one of geography, since the documentary value of Cabeza de Vaca's narrative hinged on being able to link his words to places that could be identified and recognized. This explains the copious bibliography that has been generated over the years on the route of the Narváez expedition. In essence there have been two separate phases of interest in determining where the Narváez expeditionaries had been: one immediately following the men's return, which was driven by the desire to exploit the regions they had visited, and the other historical, commencing in the 1850s with Buckingham Smith's contemplation of the men's route for the first time in print.

Cabeza de Vaca suggests at the end of his account that the place where the expedition landed on the west coast of the Florida Peninsula became well known to the Spanish immediately after the Narváez expedition went there in 1528, presumably due to the search effort launched from Cuba to locate the three hundred members of Narváez's company who had gone into the interior. The De Soto expedition explored southeastern North America extensively during the period of 1539 to 1543, and the accounts of this exploration make reference to the places where the Narváez expedition had been. However, these references to the Narváez expedition in at least some of the De Soto expedition accounts appear to be the result of the De Soto chroniclers' readings of Cabeza de Vaca's *relación* rather than manifestations of the De Soto expeditionaries' discoveries of evidence of the Narváez expeditionaries' prior presence in the regions traversed (see Adorno and Pautz 2:120–28). The De Soto expedition was followed in 1560 by the Tristán de Luna y Arellano exploration, but from then until the 1680s Spanish interest in the northern Gulf of Mexico virtually disappeared. It revived only when it was discovered that La Salle had begun to construct a fort for the French on Matagorda Bay in 1685.

When viewed in the aggregate, the geographical information that Cabeza de Vaca provided about the coast of the northern Gulf of Mexico beyond where the men disembarked was scant: a river so large that fresh water flowed swiftly into the North Sea, a series of four rivers that emptied into the North Sea and a large bay just beyond them that Cabeza de Vaca associated with the name Espíritu Santo from previous Spanish exploration, a swift river that at the point the men crossed it had a depth that reached their chests and was as wide as the one of Seville (the Río Guadalquivir), and, finally, mountains that appeared to be some fifteen leagues from the coast of the North Sea. Confusion about the identity and location of even the most significant of these geographical landmarks—the mouth of the Mississippi River—and the relationship that the name Espíritu Santo bore to the Mississippi or to Matagorda Bay, persisted into the eighteenth century. Ironically, Cabeza de Vaca's account of mountains near the Gulf Coast has been frequently ignored or discredited by investigators of his route in order to justify the hypothesis that the final four survivors of the expedition followed a direct trans-Texas route upon leaving the coast.

At the western extremes of the Narváez expedition survivors' travels, the men's return was followed by a more sustained Spanish presence in the areas they had covered. Fray Marcos de Niza explored the region with Estevanico as his guide in 1538. This exploration was followed by the extensive Coronado and Alarcón explorations of 1540–42, the Francisco de Ibarra expedition of 1565, the Rodríguez-Chamuscado expedition of 1581, and the Antonio de Espejo expedition of 1583. The reporters of these expeditions invoked a typically distant and vague memory of the Narváez expeditionaries in their accounts but, as with the De Soto chronicles, the source of the influence was likely to have been a textual one rather than any decipherable mark that the Narváez survivors had left on the land or in the collective memory of the native peoples they had encountered (see Adorno and Pautz 3:129–35, 141–50). The route the men had followed along the coastal corridor from Corazones to the Río Sinaloa (Río Petatlán; see map 1) was followed by Coronado, but beyond that point no landmarks identified by Cabeza de Vaca were sufficiently described such that subsequent expeditions were able to confirm without doubt that Cabeza de Vaca had been there. Most significantly, Cabeza de Vaca brought news of sedentary agricultural peoples. Knowledge from Coronado's explorations quickly eclipsed the more rudimentary information that Cabeza de Vaca's account could offer.

With the passage of nearly five hundred years the delicate referential links of Cabeza de Vaca's text to the physical world he experienced become more fragile, and aspects of that physical world have ceased to exist. Geography, presumably the most stable element to which the account attaches itself, experiences natural and human modification of the landscape that Cabeza de Vaca traversed. The island, inlet, or bay that Cabeza de Vaca described in the 1530s may no longer exist today. We are conscious of this fact in making geographical identifications in this edition, no matter how specific we attempt to make them. Even more volatile are the continued existence and current ranges of the flora and fauna that Cabeza de Vaca described. We have made every effort to consider the potential changes to the natural habitats of the bison and the prickly pear cactus that have occurred since the 1520s and 1530s in our use of this information to establish the route that the Narváez expeditionaries followed. Fortunately, the novelty of the opossum, the bison, the prickly pear cactus, and mesquite compelled Cabeza de Vaca to write about them in such a way that our continued modern-day familiarity with them makes them immediately recognizable in his text. Whether the bison will still symbolize some surviving notion of the American West or the opossum will still be ubiquitous to North America another five hundred years from now remains to be seen.

Without question, the most charged interpretative impulse with regard to Cabeza de Vaca's text has been to associate the Amerindian peoples that he encountered in the 1520s and 1530s with tribal groups identified decades or even more than a century later. With regard to the Amerindians of the Texas coast, whom Cabeza de Vaca described in the greatest detail, no extant ethnographic information about the inhabitants of this region was generated after Cabeza de Vaca's 1542 account until at least the end of the seventeenth century. Identifying the groups that Cabeza de Vaca had encountered at Malhado as Karankawa, a group not identified until the eighteenth century, denies the certain transformation, if not elimination, of the peoples with whom Cabeza de Vaca had lived. For this reason we have excluded all such retrospective associations in our annotation of Cabeza de Vaca's account. Gerhard's (344) observation about the area of present-day northern Nuevo León, Mexico, is instructive:

> After Cabeza de Vaca, I find no significant ethnohistorical material from Nuevo León earlier than the history of Alonso de León, who reported on conditions as he saw them between 1636 and 1650. During the intervening century the original inhabitants, decimated by disease and violence, many of them transported to the Zacatecas mines, were to a certain extent replaced by people from outside the area, and thus León's observations may not be entirely or at all applicable to the situation at first Spanish contact. However, the scanty archaeological evidence points to cultural continuity in those years.

Finally, Cabeza de Vaca's account bears witness to the immense potential for presumably obvious and stable points of reference to be misunderstood.

As was typical of all chronicles of exploration, the reporters of expeditions exploited the familiar to explain the new whenever possible. Cabeza de Vaca was not unique in this regard, and he employed cultural translations to describe a river like the one of Seville, nuts the size of the ones of Galicia, fierceness of fighting among the natives of the Texas coast that approached that seen in the wars of Italy, and cattle like that of Spain. With an impressive breadth and depth of experience in the Americas, Oviedo took Cabeza de Vaca's reference to the cattle of Spain and translated it back, but incorrectly. This roundtrip cultural translation had the curious effect of transforming the American bison, which Cabeza de Vaca was the first European to describe, into a form of tapir native to Central America. Once Oviedo received reports of the bison from the Coronado expedition he corrected his own misunderstanding (see Adorno and Pautz 2:226–35).

These cultural translations are likewise subject to the ravages of time. In a description of the distribution of native dwellings in the region of Apalache, Cabeza de Vaca reported that they were "scattered about the countryside in the same manner as those of Gelves." At least since 1945 this reference in Cabeza de Vaca's *relación* has been identified as the island of Djerba off the coast of Tunisia, and the reference in the celebrated sixteenth-century Spanish literary classic *Lazarillo de Tormes* to one of the two Spanish military campaigns to the island in 1510 or 1520 is well known. Nevertheless, most modern editions of the *relación* have associated the reference in Cabeza de Vaca's text with a small Andalusian town located south of Seville, on the basis of name alone. In his 1526 *Descrizione dell'Africa*, Joannes Leo Africanus said that the island's inhabitants "live in hamlets of which the houses are dispersed, each property having its own house inhabited by a single family. Yet there are also certain of these hamlets where the houses are grouped together" (400). Knowledge of the island of Djerba must already have seemed obscure by the 1540s. When Alonso de Santa Cruz paraphrased a version of Cabeza de Vaca's *Florida* account (see "Oviedo's and Santa Cruz's Histories"), he transformed the Gelves reference to "the houses [are] scattered through the countryside in the fashion of the farmsteads [*caseríos*] of the Basque country [Vizcaya]," evidently assuming that the latter reference would more clearly convey the meaning of Cabeza de Vaca's statement (see Adorno and Pautz 2:127–31).

If the problem of reference confounded readers in Cabeza de Vaca's day, it is no surprise that it continues to do so in our own. Whether the referent is lost in time or absent in space, or both, the challenge now as then is to make connections from the word to the world that stands outside the text (or to refrain from doing so) while avoiding precipitous or arbitrary assumptions about that world or the author's apprehension of it. To Cabeza de Vaca as author, the intellectual, linguistic, and rhetorical challenges were self-evident. Even before inviting his primary reader, the emperor, to open his report, he cautioned that although some matters he discussed were so novel as to seem unsusceptible to belief, they should be given credence (f2v). Contained in his statement is not only his obvious insistence on his fidelity to the truth but also his desire to have conveyed as accurately as possible the reality of what he had seen and experienced. To observe his approach to this complex challenge is one of the many sources of fascination in reading the *relación*.

Recording the Narváez Expedition Experience

After the four survivors' arrival in México-Tenochtitlán in July 1536, oral accounts of the Cabeza de Vaca journey raised new hopes about future exploration, settlement, and evangelization. On at least one occasion the four men were reported as having appeared at the principal church of the newly colonized México-Tenochtitlán, "dressed in skins, just as they had arrived from the land of *Florida*" (AGI, Patronato 57, no. 4, ramo 1, f11r). The scene suggests the excitement of the news they brought, the conversations that ensued, and the expectations that would be generated. One of their interlocutors during their stay in New Spain's capital was its first archbishop, the Franciscan Fray Juan de Zumárraga. Zumárraga (91) relied on his conversations with the four men to provide guidance for the peaceful conversion of the natives; he was apparently convinced that the natives had treated the four men "better than if they themselves were already Christian" and that they had held them "in as much veneration as we do the saints."

However their experiences were interpreted by others, the survivors had their own solemn task to perform. It was the duty of the three Castilians to prepare an official account of their experiences in the king's service. (As a slave, Estevanico's legal testimony was not invited.) Their sworn testimony was gathered and signed collectively by them between the end of July and the beginning of October 1536, when Cabeza de Vaca first attempted to return to Spain. This written account, the so-called Joint Report, was submitted to the viceroy of New Spain, Antonio de Mendoza, as well as to the Audiencia of Santo Domingo, the highest governing body of the jurisdiction that included the lands of *Florida*. The Joint Report is the most significant account of the Narváez expedition, and it is now lost.

It was from the Audiencia of Santo Domingo that Gonzalo Fernández de Oviedo y Valdés received a copy of the Joint Report, and on its basis he wrote his account of the expedition and its survivors in his *Historia general y natural de las Indias* (book 35, chaps. 1–7). Oviedo's (3:615a) reference to the Joint Report as "the first *relación*" and to Cabeza de Vaca's published account as "the second *relación*" testifies to the primacy of the Joint Report as the initial, and official, survivors' account of the Narváez expedition and its aftermath.

Oviedo's remark anticipates and underscores an important point: Cabeza de Vaca's narrative is a retrospective, highly inflected personal account of his and his companions' experiences. Oviedo's careful reading of the Joint Report, his use of it in constructing his own account of the Narváez expedition, and his incorporation of an additional chapter after reading Cabeza de Vaca's 1542 published *relación* make his narration our best source for corroborating, clarifying, or contradicting claims made by Cabeza de Vaca. Oviedo's text offers the only access to independent testimony given by Andrés Dorantes pertaining to the period between the spring of 1529 and the summer of 1534, during which time Cabeza de Vaca and the other three survivors were separated, except for a brief period in the summer of 1533 (see Adorno and Pautz 3:12–45). Because of its corroborative and evaluative qualities, we make frequent reference to Oviedo's work in the annotation to this edition.

Cabeza de Vaca's 1542 *relación* is the last link in a chain of reports that he had written during and after the expedition. We reconstruct that documentary sequence in order to set in relief his later, more mediated efforts in writing the *relación*. Cabeza de Vaca's charge to report on the course of the expedition had begun with his royal appointment as its chief treasury official. His formal instructions from the emperor on 15 February 1527, signed by Francisco de los Cobos as royal secretary of the Councils of Castile and of the Indies, acting on the emperor's behalf, were as follows:

> Also, you will take great care of, and be diligent to look after everything that may tend to our service and which should be done in that country or the neighboring islands, for their peopling and pacification, informing us extensively and particularly of every matter, especially of how our commands are obeyed and executed in those lands and provinces, of how the natives are treated, our instructions observed, and other of the things respecting their liberties that we have commanded; especially the matters touching the service of our Lord and divine worship, the teachings of the Indians in the Holy Faith, and in many other things of our service, as well as all the rest you see, and I should be informed of. (AGI, Casa de la Contratación 3309, 32–4-29/35, f 36v; Smith, *Relation* 221)

Given his official responsibilities for reporting on the expedition, his references in the *relación* to making reports to the emperor corresponded to the direct line of his duties.

We know about the one-time existence of four documents that Cabeza de Vaca had a hand in preparing or for which he provided testimony during the course of the expedition and its trans–Texas-Mexico aftermath. Two letters, written by Cabeza de Vaca to the emperor and dated 28 November 1527 and 15 February 1528, from Jagua (Cienfuegos), Cuba, reported on the progress of the expedition and testified to the loss of ships, men, and horses in the November 1527 hurricane in Cuba. A *probanza*, or compilation of sworn and certified oral testimonies recorded in writing, was produced at the same time. It provided various men's accounts of the hurricane and the losses occasioned by it. Finally, a sworn statement, dated in the spring of 1536, certified the four overland survivors' arrival at the Río Petatlán (modern Río Sinaloa) and their reunion with Spanish soldiers in Nueva Galicia in northwestern Mexico. These four documents are now lost, but a letter in the Archivo General de Indias in Seville, Spain, written by the emperor to Cabeza de Vaca on 27 March 1528, acknowledged receipt of the letter from Jagua written on 28 November 1527. The evidence of the existence of the other three reports comes from Oviedo's and Cabeza de Vaca's references to them in their published accounts (see Adorno and Pautz 3:8–12).

After the men's arrival in the capital of New Spain and their preparation of the Joint Report, Cabeza de Vaca and Andrés Dorantes prepared another document in late 1536 or early 1537 whose specific contents are unknown but which undoubtedly represented the interests of the two of them. Cabeza de Vaca presented this petition to the emperor at court in Valladolid at the end of 1537; it too is lost (see Adorno and Pautz 3:45–50).

Writing the *Relación* to the Emperor (1538–40)

When Cabeza de Vaca arrived at court in Valladolid in late 1537, he discovered that he was too late to bid for the contract for the governorship of *Florida*, which had been granted to Hernando de Soto just ten days after Cabeza de Vaca had departed Veracruz for Spain in April 1537. Now meeting De Soto at court, Cabeza de Vaca turned down the new appointee's invitation to serve under his command. It was at this time, after the end of 1537 when he was back in Spain, that Cabeza de Vaca sat down to write the *relación* that would be published in 1542. Undoubtedly working on the basis of his testimony in the Joint Report and possibly relying on his joint petition with Dorantes, Cabeza de Vaca produced his now-famous, comprehensive account between the beginning of 1538 and some point in 1540 (see Adorno and Pautz 3:52–67).

In contrast to the previous written and oral reports in which he had recounted his *Florida* experience, Cabeza de Vaca's 1542 *relación* was the first to represent his interests alone. His immediate purpose was to present his account as a kind of "narrative curriculum vitae" in support of his petition for another royal contract for exploration and conquest in the Indies. He achieved this goal in early 1540 when he was granted the governorship of the province of Río de la Plata in modern Paraguay, South America, and given the military command (*adelantamiento*) of any additional lands that he might discover, conquer, and settle (Vas Mingo 362–66). He set sail from Cádiz with four ships and a company of four hundred men on 2 December 1540, and his *relación* appeared in print in Zamora with an official publication date of 6 October 1542 (see Adorno and Pautz 3:67–75).

Cabeza de Vaca directed his published *relación* explicitly to Charles V, just as his 1527 and 1528 expedition letters from Cuba and his 1537 joint petition with Dorantes had been. In the proem Cabeza de Vaca dedicated the work to his sovereign and addressed him on several occasions throughout the course of the narrative. The importance of the emperor as the work's primary recipient and reader is graphically represented on the frontispiece of the 1542 printing (see figure). It features Charles V's imperial coat of arms instead of the author's, which the account potentially might have borne had the work been destined for a general readership (see Adorno and Pautz 1:333–40; 3:55–58). (The 1555 edition's frontispiece also emphasizes Cabeza de Vaca's life in his king's service through its use of imperial heraldry.)

The immediate purpose of Cabeza de Vaca's 1542 account was to describe the services he had performed on the monarch's behalf. Since, however, he could not boast of offering the crown economic gain in the customary forms of lands or peoples conquered or mineral wealth revealed, he presented the emperor the only thing he had acquired in the Indies: remarkable new information about the unknown lands and peoples to the north of New Spain. He emphasized this point in his proem:

> I had no opportunity to perform greater service than this, which is to bring to Your Majesty an account of all that I was able to observe and learn in the nine years that I walked lost and naked through many and very strange lands, as much regarding the locations of the lands and provinces and the distances among them, as with respect to the foodstuffs and animals that are produced in them, and the diverse customs of many and very barbarous peoples with whom I conversed and lived, plus all the other particularities that I could come to know and understand, so that in some manner Your Majesty may be served. (f2r)

The pragmatic purpose of his account is apparent. At the same time, Cabeza de Vaca's acknowledgment of the novelty and apparent incredibility of the events and customs he described ("I wrote all this with such sure knowledge that although some very novel things may be read in it, very difficult for

Frontispiece of the 1542
Zamora edition of Cabeza
de Vaca's *Relación* (f1r).
Courtesy of the Rare Books
and Manuscripts Division,
The New York Public
Library, Astor, Lenox, and
Tilden Foundations.

Ⓒ La relacion que dio Aluar nu=
ñez cabeça de vaca de lo acaescido enlas Indias
enla armada donde yua por gouernador pā
philo de narbaez desde el año de veynte
y siete hasta el año ð treynta y seys
que boluio a Sevilla con tres
de su compañia.:.

some to believe, they can absolutely give them credence"), as well as his
expressed certitude that "all men desire to know the customs and practices
of others" emphasized his awareness of the play of the reader's intellectual
curiosity for its own sake (f2v, f43v–f44r).

Cabeza de Vaca had much opportunity to reflect upon, and retell, his
experiences during the eight months he spent in the Mexican capital waiting
to return to Spain, during the four-month-long sea voyage home, and over
the course of the long months or even year or more afterward in Castile. As

a result, in writing his narrative he attempted not merely to recall all that had happened but also to narrate it in a compelling manner, underscoring its affective significance.

Within the constraints of formality and decorum imposed in writing to his sovereign, Cabeza de Vaca conveyed sentiments that potentially could have a strong effect on his reader. He could not have been unaware of the high drama he created in portraying the protagonism of events by Pánfilo de Narváez and himself at a crucial moment when the five rafts coasted the uncertain waters of the Gulf of Mexico and the men were stricken by starvation and thirst. He wrote that Narváez had answered his query about what should be done in such straits by announcing that "it was no longer time for one man to rule another, that each one should do whatever seemed best to him in order to save his own life" (f20r). Later, the healing episodes ("the wonders that our Lord was working through us") are created as scenes of solemn, initially tense encounter that eventually tumble over and into one another, carrying the four men forward across northern Mexico and southwestern Texas at a breathtaking pace: "opening roads for us through a land so deserted, bringing us people where many times there were none, and liberating us from so many dangers and not permitting us to be killed" (f35v–f36r).

Equally dramatically, Cabeza de Vaca portrayed the initial period after the four men's reunion with their countrymen as one of bitter irony. The return to civilization brought not the desired liberty but rather its loss. The four survivors were moved along under the armed escort of Spanish soldiers to keep them from conversation with the Indians whom they had reassured and sent away in peace but whom the soldiers now planned to attack. "From which it is evident," Cabeza de Vaca remarked, "how much men's thoughts deceive them, for we went to them seeking liberty and when we thought we had it, it turned out to be so much to the contrary" (f60v).

Among the small but suggestive interpretive keys placed in the reader's path are Cabeza de Vaca's exploitation of the miracle of the burning bush when he was lost in the wilderness for five days, his reference to the martyrdom of Jesus Christ to describe his own sufferings, and his framing of the entire narration with an event that he said had occurred before the expedition set out, namely, the prophecy of the Muslim woman from Hornachos that projected doom for many and great wealth for those who survived (f36v, f40v, f65v–f66r).

The reader is prompted to ask: Was the outcome of the Narváez expedition, then, in Cabeza de Vaca's view, an ineludible destiny? Was it fate or fortune? Was it the inscrutable will of God? Cabeza de Vaca leaves the reader with all these choices at the head and foot of his account. In his proem to the emperor, which can sustain as many readings as the interested reader can give it, he remarked, "beyond the particular advantage that any one can secure for himself, there is a very great disparity not caused by the shortcoming of any one of them, but only by fortune, or more certainly through no fault of one's own, but only by the will and judgment of God" (fiv). Yet at the very end of his work he concluded his account of the Muslim woman's prophecy with the statement, "and the entire voyage had occurred to us in the same manner that she had told us" (f66r). The great conundrum of his understanding of his experience seems to have been that, as left to the devising of human will, things turned out so much better, and at the same time so much worse, than he would have anticipated.

Cabeza de Vaca's *relación* is thus at one and the same time a documentary account of a lived experience and an attempt to interpret it. It is the endeavor to come to grips with a seemingly incredible experience (Cabeza de Vaca cautioned his imperial reader that such a reading would be possible but wrong) and to recount extraordinary but natural occurrences. How could they be explained at a higher level? Cabeza de Vaca's alternate, searching references to the will of the Christian God and the superstitious prophecy of the non-Christian Extremaduran woman do not give us his answer to the question, but they do reveal the seriousness of his effort to address it. The earnestness of this effort at interpretation and explanation reveals the *relación* for what it is: an account of the vexing paradoxes that characterize human experience.

Oviedo's and Santa Cruz's Histories of the Narváez Expedition

During this same period of the early 1540s and with no knowledge of Cabeza de Vaca's *relación* but with the Joint Report in hand, Oviedo y Valdés wrote his account of the Narváez expedition. It ultimately became chapters one through six of book thirty-five of his *Historia general y natural de las Indias*.

In 1547 Oviedo met Cabeza de Vaca at Prince Philip's court in Madrid, and he urged Cabeza de Vaca to show him the printed *relación*. After studying it and when writing chapter seven of book thirty-five of his *Historia* on its basis at the end of that year or by mid-January 1548, Oviedo (3:614a–15a) declared that he could vouch for Cabeza de Vaca's credibility because of his eyewitness participation in the events narrated and because his account was corroborated by the Joint Report that Oviedo himself had studied. Oviedo's preference for the collective report of the three men over Cabeza de Vaca's published account reminds us that, as a historian, Oviedo's chief interest was the men's common experience and their mutually corroborated testimony about the nature of the lands they had visited and the customs of the peoples they had encountered.

There is another account, known as the Short Report, that is often misunderstood as having been authored by Cabeza de Vaca and thus is erroneously considered to be part of the ensemble of original documents of the Narváez expedition. It is, instead, a partial but imperfect paraphrase of Cabeza de Vaca's account, either taken directly from the 1542 published *relación* or from one of the manuscript versions that had served as its source. Written sometime in the 1540s, it is known today in a copy made at the end of the eighteenth century by the great Spanish archival historian Juan Bautista Muñoz, who annotated it "De Santa Cruz, de los papeles de Sevilla" (By Santa Cruz, from the Seville papers). It recounts the events of the Narváez expedition's fate from April 1528 to the spring of 1533, that is, from the expedition's arrival in *Florida* on the west coast of the Florida Peninsula through its survivors' sojourn in the region of the Texas coastal island of Malhado in Galveston Bay.

The number of errors in the Short Report's transcription, which consist of misidentifying Cabeza de Vaca as "Vaca de Castro," calling the makeshift rafts by the name of a specific type of craft of European manufacture, and erring on the basic data about the expedition, all make it impossible for Cabeza de Vaca to have been its author. It is instead the work of Alonso de Santa Cruz, the royal chronicler and cosmographer of Charles V, who copied out its information about the lands of *Florida* and their exploration in his capacity as cosmographer (see Adorno and Pautz 3:75–81).

Sometime before 1551, under his charge as royal chronicler, Santa Cruz wrote an account of the Narváez expedition as part of his *Crónica del emperador Carlos V*. Here he also used as his source a manuscript account very similar in language and content to Cabeza de Vaca's 1542 *relación* and/or the published 1542 text itself. Our discovery of the account of the Narváez expedition in Santa Cruz's history of the reign of Charles V corroborates Muñoz's observation that the Short Report was likely to have been penned by Santa Cruz (see Adorno and Pautz 3:81–83). After Oviedo, Santa Cruz was the second historian to write an account of the Narváez expedition for a work of Spanish history, and he would be followed by Francisco López de Gómara and his *Historia general de las Indias* (1552).

Destined for a Broader Readership (*Relación y comentarios*)

In 1555 Cabeza de Vaca published in Valladolid his *Relación y comentarios*, that is, the republication of his account of his North American odyssey of 1527–36, along with the first-time appearance of the "commentaries" or the account of his 1541–45 governorship of Río de la Plata, authored by the secretary of the province, his aide, Pero Hernández.

The relationship of the 1555 republication of the *relación* to its 1542 source is not that of a "definitive work" to its "preliminary version." Both publications share the same content, and the second version is not any more "polished" grammatically, syntactically, or stylistically than the first. They are instead works seeking different readerships and serving different purposes, and these differences are conveyed by the framing documents and narrative formats in which the *Florida* account is presented.

The 1542 *relación* offers an account of services rendered and presents a petition for recognition that beseeches a favorable disposition from its royal reader. It demands its reader's uninterrupted attention and conveys the immediacy and urgency of a report meant to be taken up in a single reading. To the emperor Cabeza de Vaca described his report as being "brief rather than lengthy," and he asked that it be received "in the name of service, because this alone is what a man who came away naked could carry out with him" (f2v).

In contrast, he cast the 1555 account with a broader range of readers in mind. It is divided into chapters with descriptive titles, thus inviting a leisurely reading as a book to be picked up and put down at will. Its purpose, in combination with that of its companion text, the *Comentarios*, was to delight the reader. To the young prince Don Carlos, the son of Prince Philip to whom he dedicated his 1555 book, Cabeza de Vaca remarked that he had assembled the accounts of *Florida* and Río de la Plata under the same cover so that the variety of matters treated in one and the other might serve to bring pleasure to the prince (Serrano y Sanz 1:148).

Variety, as an aesthetic value, was achieved. Taken together the North and South American narratives provided the princely or other armchair traveler of the sixteenth century with a breathtaking sweep of lands and peoples of the northern and southern reaches of Spain's far-flung American empire and its viceroyalties of New Spain and Peru. It embraced at one extreme the territories beyond the northern boundaries of the former Aztec confederation of Mexico and, at the other, the lands to the south of the Incas' imperial Tawantinsuyu.

Cabeza de Vaca had already acknowledged the delight of the spectacle of the variety of lands and customs in his 1542 *relación*. Emphasizing this aspect in his 1555 proem to prince Don Carlos, he added as another object of readerly interest the vicissitudes of human fate: "It is certainly true that there is nothing that more delights readers than the variety of deeds and times and reversals of fortune, which, although at the time they are experienced are not pleasant, become agreeable when we recall them in memory and read about them" (Serrano y Sanz 1:148). The contrast between the proem addressed to the emperor in the 1542 edition and the one directed to the emperor's grandson in the 1555 republication is revealing. To the emperor in 1542 Cabeza de Vaca offered strategic information to be used as a basis for action. Thirteen years later to the young Don Carlos he offered the variety of landscapes and customs for the pleasure of their diversity. Beyond his 1542 emphasis on the documentary value of his geographic and ethnographic information, Cabeza de Vaca appreciated in 1555 the refraction of the images of his experience made possible by the passage of time and removal in distance. Cabeza de Vaca himself thus anticipated the modern readings of his *relación* when he invoked the variety of human custom and the twists of human fate that had the power to entertain readers and invite their philosophical speculation on life's enigmas.

Sixteenth- to Eighteenth-Century Readers of the *Relación*

Cabeza de Vaca's oral accounts and the gossip at court helped foster other Spanish expeditions into the unknown north in the quixotic search for such wonders as the "Seven Cities of Cíbola." After his own return from the De Soto expedition, the Gentleman of Elvas recalled Cabeza de Vaca's visit to the court in Valladolid in 1537 and remembered that Cabeza de Vaca's report had led the men there assembled to believe that the country that he had visited and that they were about to experience was the richest in the world. The Gentleman of Elvas added that Cabeza de Vaca's report was so compelling that all the men of good breeding who had sold their estates and volunteered for the De Soto expedition simply could not be accommodated on the ships waiting in port at Sanlúcar de Barrameda (Clayton, Knight, and Moore 1:48).

Among the first eager readers of Cabeza de Vaca's published *relación*, therefore, we are not surprised to find Spanish explorers and conquistadors of the De Soto and Coronado expeditions. As mentioned above, De Soto expedition reporters recounting their 1539–43 experiences in the 1540s and 1550s, and Coronado expedition writers giving accounts of their 1540–42 sojourn in the 1560s, drafted accounts of their own experiences that were colored by their direct or indirect knowledge of Cabeza de Vaca's *relación*. In the same decades the erudite historians of Spain's overseas empire— Oviedo, Santa Cruz, and Gómara—all read and relied on Cabeza de Vaca's account. The *Apologética Historia Sumaria*, Las Casas's great treatise on the universality of the exercise of human reason as characteristic of all the world's cultures, relied heavily on Cabeza de Vaca's account for information about the native inhabitants of the lands north of New Spain.

A very special case is offered by El Inca Garcilaso de la Vega's *La Florida del Inca* ([1587] 1605), which provided one of the most complex and compelling readings of Cabeza de Vaca of the period. Garcilaso's literary reconstruction of the De Soto expedition at its points of convergence with the Narváez expedition was based on information he drew from the 1555 edition of Cabeza de Vaca's *relación*. His embellishment of it relied both on Cabeza de Vaca's narrative and on one or more of the earlier De Soto expedition accounts, which in turn had already been influenced by Cabeza de Vaca's narrative (see Adorno and Pautz 2:122–27; 3:129–44, 150–54).

Missionaries founding new settlements in Spanish North America, explorers opening the northern lands, and governors of outlying northern Spanish provinces all had the reports of Cabeza de Vaca and his three companions as reference points on their historical and cultural maps of the expansion of Spanish civilization. Although we can perceive a broad trend from historicizing to mythologizing the Narváez survivors' experience, there was no single, monolithic body of linearly evolving interpretation produced by the chronological trajectory of readings. As far as trends go, the main one was identified by Jacques Lafaye, that is, the tendency to portray the deeds of the men as miraculous.

Yet the healing episodes as such give us but one dimension of the interpretive history of the Cabeza de Vaca story, whose significance has also been configured more broadly. The casting of the four men as founders and civilizers of lands to the northwest and northeast of New Spain became a prominent theme that identified them as the "Adam" of the Spanish presence on the northern frontier and the "Moses" of the native peoples to the north of New Spain. In this manner the sixteenth- through eighteenth-century readings grafted civic and patrimonial impulses onto the religious initiative. Thus the universal goals of the Spanish empire (territorial expansion and religious conversion) were subtly transformed into the harbingers—even in the word's archaic sense as "people sent ahead to provide lodgings"—of regional identity (see Adorno and Pautz 3:161–66, 170–71).

While Cabeza de Vaca's *relación* was cited by readers with geographical and political interest in Spain, such as the royal chronicler and cosmographer of the Indies, Juan López de Velasco, it was also being translated and commented upon for similar reasons by writers representing rival powers abroad. The Italian states in the 1550s and England in the early seventeenth century provide notable examples. Through translation into Italian by Gian Battista Ramusio in 1556, mention by Richard Hakluyt in 1609 in his *Virginia Richly Valued by the Description of the Maine Land of Florida Her Next Neighbour*, and subsequent paraphrase into English and publication in Samuel Purchas's 1625 *Purchas his Pilgrimes*, Cabeza de Vaca's account fed the imagination of the earliest English colonists regarding the lands they were going to settle along the Atlantic seaboard of North America (see Adorno and Pautz 3:140–45, 158–60).

Modern Re-editions of the *Relación* and New Readerships

The modern readings of Cabeza de Vaca's account began in the eighteenth century with Andrés González de Barcia's republication of the 1555 text of the *relación* in Madrid in 1731. He entitled it "Naufragios de Álvar Núñez Cabeza de Vaca, y relación de la jornada que hizo a la Florida con el adelantado Pánfilo de Narváez" (The Misfortunes of Álvar Núñez Cabeza de Vaca and the Account of the Journey that He Took to Florida with the Military Commander Pánfilo de Narváez). This was the first use of "Naufragios" (calamities; misfortunes; shipwrecks) as the work's title, although it had first appeared as the running head at the top of the folios and on the table of contents of the 1555 edition. Barcia printed the *Naufragios* as part of his in-progress project of collecting and publishing accounts of Spanish exploration and settlement in the Americas. The purpose of his *Historiadores primitivos de las Indias Occidentales* (Early Historians of the Occidental Indies) was to rehabilitate the historical reputation of Spain in the face of the widely circulating "Black Legend" characterization of Spanish history as cruel and tyrannical. Inasmuch as Cabeza de Vaca's account countered the image of bloody conquest, proposed a program of peaceful colonization and evangelization, and, most important, portrayed the terms of the European-Amerindian engagement humane and even "spiritual," it is not surprising that Barcia selected it for one of his early printings. The companion piece he chose to publish with it underscores these objectives.

In Barcia's edition the *relación* was accompanied not by Pero Hernández's "commentaries" on Cabeza de Vaca's governorship of Río de la Plata, but rather by an erudite treatise and scholarly defense of the miraculous curings presumably performed by Cabeza de Vaca and his companions: Antonio Ardoino's *Examen apologético de la histórica narración de los naufragios, peregrinaciones i milagros de Álvar Núñez Cabeza de Baca en las tierras de la Florida, i del Nuevo México* (A Vindicating Examination of the Historical Narration of the Calamities, Peregrinations, and Miracles of Álvar Núñez Cabeza de Vaca in the Lands of Florida and New Mexico). When in 1749 the three-volume *Historiadores primitivos* was published in full, Cabeza de Vaca's *relación* and Ardoino's *Examen apologético* were again side by side (see Adorno and Pautz 3:177–89).

Barcia did not make a deliberate choice of the 1555 text over the 1542 edition. He simply had been unaware of its existence until a few years after his 1731 publication. His effort, nevertheless, had the effect of privileging the 1555 text over that of 1542, as well as fixing its title as *Naufragios* and fomenting the *a posteriori* development of arguments intended to vindicate the supposed superiority of the 1555 edition. Hence, Barcia's default election of the 1555 Valladolid text as the source and format of his transcription, his use of the title *Naufragios*, and his elimination of the paratextual pieces of the work were canonized when Enrique de Vedia reedited Barcia's *Historiadores primitivos* for its inclusion as volume twenty-two of the *Biblioteca de Autores Españoles* in 1852 (see Adorno and Pautz 3:189–90). Vedia's action had a lasting effect, and the 1555 text or transcriptions of it have been the basis for every erudite and popular Spanish-language edition of the work to this day, with the exception of our recent 1999 edition of Cabeza de Vaca's originally published 1542 text (Adorno and Pautz 1:14–278).

We close this essay with reference to the eighteenth-century "reader" with whom we began: Thomas Jefferson. The account of the Spanish conquistador Cabeza de Vaca's North American sojourn has a long reach that carries forward Jefferson's vision of a hemispheric America and its transatlantic coordinates. It has, furthermore, never been forgotten in Cabeza de Vaca's homeland, being published up to the present day in Spain as it is in Latin America and the United States. Cabeza de Vaca's modest report to the emperor Charles V has long been a staple in Spanish and Spanish American reading traditions, and that interest has been evidenced most recently by the 1990 coproduction by the Instituto Mexicano de Cinematografía and Televisión Española of Mexican filmmaker Nicolás Echevarría's feature-length film, "Cabeza de Vaca" (see Sheridan).

The quiet but steady U.S. interest that began in the middle of the nineteenth century has recently been renewed and expanded: in 1993 the "Recovering the U.S. Hispanic Literary Heritage" project, designed as a "national endeavor to reconstitute the literary legacy of U.S. Hispanics from colonial times to 1960," published Cabeza de Vaca's *relación* as the second volume in its series (Favata and Fernández). In 1994 *The Norton Anthology of American Literature* inaugurated a new section, "Literature to 1620," in which an abridgement of Cabeza de Vaca's account was anthologized, and it has appeared in each successive edition (Baym). In 1997 *The Norton Anthology of African American Literature* made a significant but indirect reference to the Narváez expedition and the *relación* in its chronology, "African American Literature in Context." It cites 1526 (which, correctly, should be 1527) as the year when the first African slaves were "brought to what is now the United States by the Spanish" (Gates and McKay 2612). Cabeza de Vaca's *relación* has been claimed, in other words, as an early landmark in Spanish-American, U.S. Anglo-American, Latino-American, and African-American cultural traditions.

In appropriating the Spanish literary heritage to the Americas, Cabeza de Vaca's *relación* has been assimilated to the Spanish-speaking tradition from its European roots in the Byzantine novel and Mediterranean fiction to its celebrated contemporary Latin American novelists (Pupo-Walker). In the United States it has been appropriated for its account of the inception of the European presence in North America, as well as its dramatization of the European encounter with native cultural and racial traditions and its portrayal of the "American" journey of territorial exploration and self-discovery (Davenport and Wells; Pilkington; Smith). In the Latino- and Hispanic-American traditions of the United States it has been heralded for antedating the English presence in North America and for providing deeply resonant perspectives on linguistic and cultural mediation (Bruce-Novoa; Favata and Fernández; Leal). The U.S. African-American tradition finds it notable for its unique portrayal of the black African historical presence and protagonism in the prehistory of the United States (Alves; Panger; Parish). Instead of canceling out one another, these disparate claims enhance the interpretive richness that Cabeza de Vaca's account affords. Given the interest it generates in various contexts in this hemisphere and on this continent, the work is American in the broadest possible sense.

What makes the work resonant to these many constituencies of readers? The larger principles that transcend the particular man and his specific historical experience include the dramatization of the protagonist's locus at the intersection between or among different, if not opposing, groups and cultures, as well as the processes of mediation across boundaries that he carries out in the course of the narrative. Both phenomena have come to be seen as fundamental to the American experience.

Most "American" of all is the fact that the account is one of personal testimony. The first voices that spoke in European languages from the islands and continents of the Americas spoke for themselves, that is, on their own behalf. Begun five hundred years ago by the Spanish, starting with Columbus's letters of his Caribbean explorations and Cortés's letters recounting his conquest of Mexico, and followed later by reports from the English and the French in North America, the firsthand account that attests to traversing the unknown and forging the new—the "self-making" of new homelands, new identities, and new futures—is the quintessence of the American experience, whatever its hemispheric geographical locale or ethnic identity.

Whether staking a claim nearly a century ago to the European heritage of the Anglo-American United States, or commemorating in the past three decades the Hispanic and Mexican American legacy in this country, or revitalizing in the past dozen years Thomas Jefferson's reference to Spanish accounts as the early part of American history, Cabeza de Vaca's *relación* has been appropriated on the basis of the linkages or "bridges" that, during his North American years at least, the historical Cabeza de Vaca constructed between various social, linguistic, cultural, and racial domains. Whether mediating between Narváez and other expeditionaries, between himself and native Amerindian groups, or, at the last, between frightened Amerindians and Spanish slave-hunters, Cabeza de Vaca gives testimony to the complexity of communication and mediation in new, untried circumstances, often without the benefit of a common language. This is the single unifying factor among all the "hyphenated" American readerships that attend to Cabeza de Vaca's account today.

In this way the seemingly remote topic of sixteenth-century Castilian experience in the Antilles and North America assumes a significant role in the U.S.-based narrative imagination from the nineteenth century into the twenty-first. The linkages or "bridges" that readers make—forging attachments to cultural experience or places of cultural origin—are all variations of the patterns at work intermittently since the days of Thomas Jefferson in bringing Columbus and Cabeza de Vaca into the multiplying narrative traditions of this continent. Whether one is interested in the topics of quest and adventure, freedom and bondage, empire and colonialism, miracles and shamanism, sacrifice and survival, transcendental good and evil, or human gain and loss, the experiences Cabeza de Vaca narrated continue to enliven readers' imaginations. Through it all, the great human mysteries at the heart of the narrative remain undisturbed.

This Edition

This edition reproduces our English translation of Cabeza de Vaca's *relación*. Both this translation and our complete, critical transcription of the original 1542 Spanish-language text on which it is based are published in Adorno and Pautz (1:14–279). Our aim in translation has been to provide the reader with a strong verbal impression in English of Cabeza de Vaca's language, conveying the texture or "feel" of the lexicon and syntactic structures he used in Spanish. Square-bracketed entries in the translation represent our introduction of words necessary for the intelligibility of the utterance. We use parentheses and dashes, however, to set off utterances given in the original text. We have introduced parentheses where Cabeza de Vaca interrupted his main utterance to interpolate relevant, often clarifying information. Dashes have been used to set off remarks by which Cabeza de Vaca added emphasis to the observations he was making. For additional information on the norms we followed in translating the Spanish-language account into English, the reader may consult Adorno and Pautz (1:3–11).

We have provided two kinds of annotation, philological and explanatory, to accompany the English-language text reproduced here:

(1) The philological annotations are cued by letters of the alphabet. They consist of: (a) the chapter titles which were inserted in the 1555 Valladolid edition of the work but had not appeared in the original 1542 Zamora edition; (b) significant variations—additions, modifications, omissions—between the 1542 and 1555 texts.

An uppercase "V" means that the item that follows it appears in the Valladolid edition. An uppercase "Z", referring to the 1542 Zamora edition, means that we have transcribed into Cabeza de Vaca's 1542 text the 1555 Valladolid item but are providing the replaced "Z" item in the note. We have made such substitutions, for example, where the Zamora text exhibited an obvious typographical error.

"V: *om.*" or "Z: *om.*" means that the 1555 Valladolid edition or the 1542 Zamora edition, respectively, omits an item that is present in the corresponding Zamora or Valladolid text.

(2) The explanatory annotations, cued by numbers, clarify or supplement information provided by Cabeza de Vaca and include geographical locations, definitions of sixteenth-century words and usages, historical references, et cetera. Many of these explanatory notes untangle the complexities of Cabeza de Vaca's seemingly straightforward prose. The most extensive series of such notes aims to make readable Cabeza de Vaca's elliptical accounts of the fates of the five rafts (f29v–f31r). All of the annotation distills the results of our investigations as developed in Adorno and Pautz (2:45–404), which the reader may consult for fuller explanations.

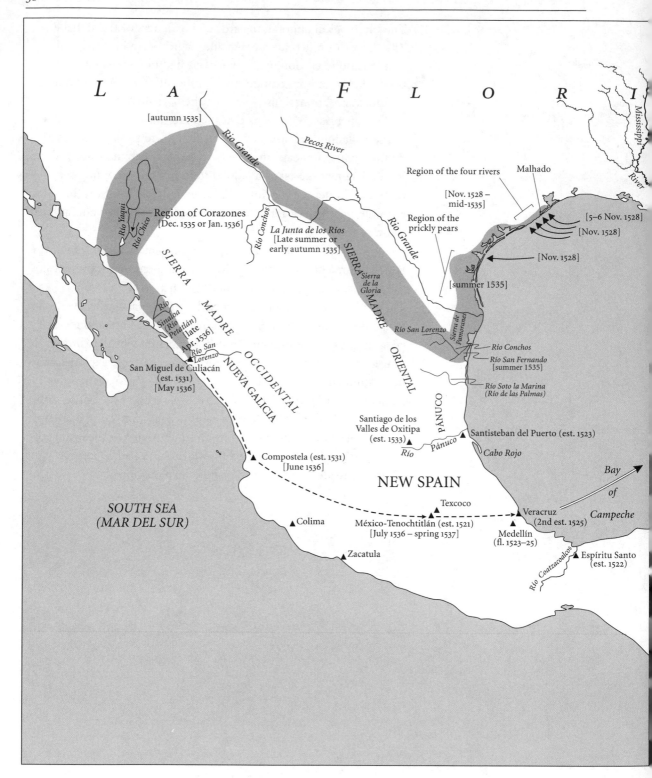

Map 1: Areas traversed by the Narváez expedition (1527 to 1528) and its four overland survivors (1528 to 1536)

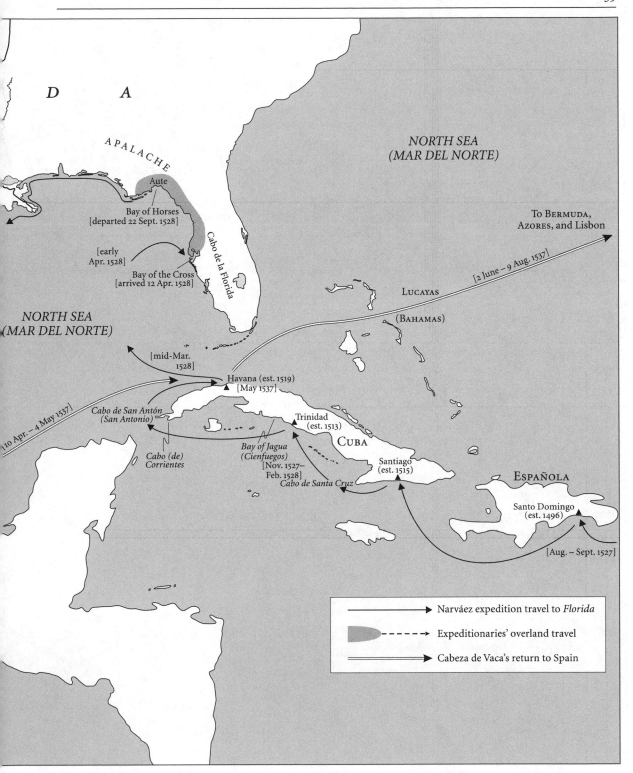

D A

APALACHE

Aute

Bay of Horses
[departed 22 Sept. 1528]

Cabo de la Florida

[early
Apr. 1528]

Bay of the Cross
[arrived 12 Apr. 1528]

NORTH SEA
(MAR DEL NORTE)

NORTH SEA
(MAR DEL NORTE)

To BERMUDA,
AZORES, and Lisbon

[2 June – 9 Aug. 1537]

LUCAYAS

(BAHAMAS)

[mid-Mar.
1528]

Havana (est. 1519)
[May 1537]

[10 Apr. – 4 May 1537]

Cabo de San Antón
(San Antonio)

Trinidad
(est. 1513)

Cabo (de)
Corrientes

Bay of Jagua
(Cienfuegos)
[Nov. 1527–
Feb. 1528]

Cabo de Santa Cruz

CUBA

Santiago
(est. 1515)

ESPAÑOLA

Santo Domingo
(est. 1496)

[Aug. – Sept. 1527]

Narváez expedition travel to *Florida*

Expeditionaries' overland travel

Cabeza de Vaca's return to Spain

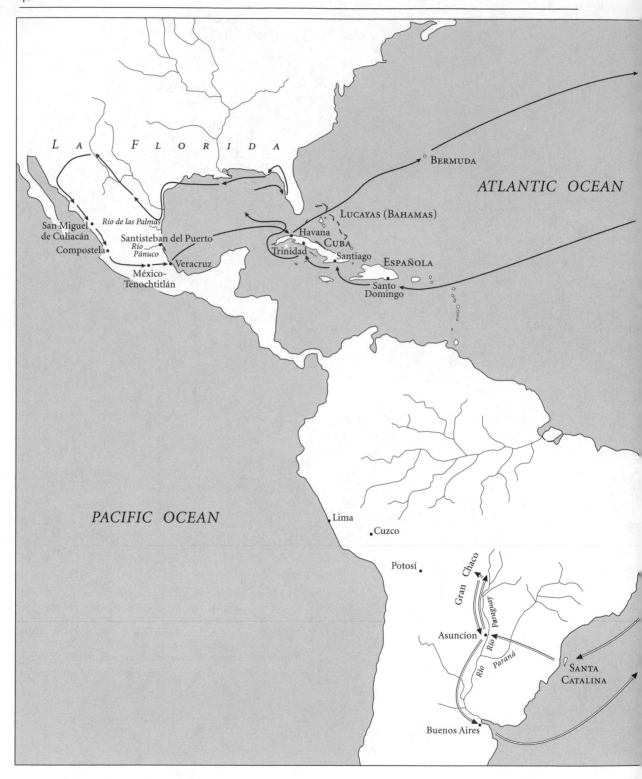

Map 2: Travels of Álvar Núñez Cabeza de Vaca (1511 to 1545)

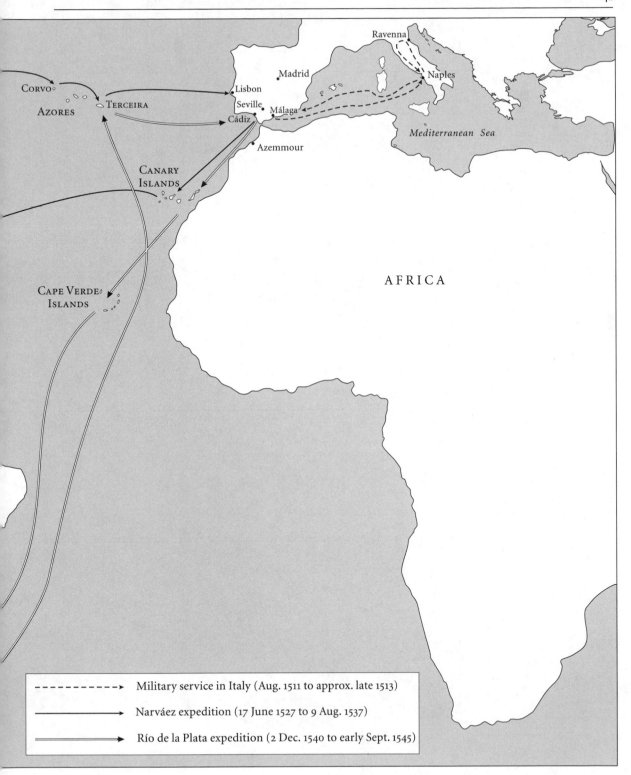

Ravenna

Madrid

Lisbon

Seville

Málaga

Cádiz

Azemmour

CORVO

AZORES

TERCEIRA

Naples

Mediterranean Sea

CANARY
ISLANDS

CAPE VERDE
ISLANDS

AFRICA

- - - - - -▶   Military service in Italy (Aug. 1511 to approx. late 1513)

──────▶   Narváez expedition (17 June 1527 to 9 Aug. 1537)

══════▶   Río de la Plata expedition (2 Dec. 1540 to early Sept. 1545)

The 1542 *Relación* (Account) of Álvar Núñez Cabeza de Vaca

a. The account . . . company.]
V: The account and com-
mentaries of Governor Álvar
Núñez Cabeza de Vaca, of what
occurred on the two journeys
he made to the Indies. By royal
authorization. Valuated by the
lords of the Council [of Castile]
at eighty-five *maravedís*.

The account that Álvar Núñez Cabeza de Vaca gave of what occurred in the Indies on the expedition of which Pánfilo de Narváez served as governor, from the year [15]27 to [15]36, when he returned to Seville with three members of his company.[a1]

1. Cabeza de Vaca returned to
Spain alone in August 1537.

Holy, Imperial, Catholic Majesty:[1]

Among as many princes as we know there have been in the world, I think none could be found whom men have tried to serve with truer will or greater diligence and desire than we see men honoring Your Majesty today. It is quite evident that this is not without great cause and reason; nor are men so ignorant that all of them blindly and arbitrarily pursue this course, since we see not only countrymen, whom faith and duty oblige to do this, but even foreigners strive to exceed their efforts. But even when the desire and will of all makes them equal in this matter, beyond the particular advantage that any one can secure for himself, there is a very great disparity not caused by the shortcoming of any one of them, but only by fortune, or more certainly through no fault of one's own, but only by the will and judgment of God, where it happens that one may come away with more notable services than he expected, while to another everything occurs so to the contrary that he cannot demonstrate any greater witness to his intention than his diligence, and even this is sometimes so obscured that it cannot make itself evident. For myself I can say that on the expedition that by command of Your Majesty I made to the mainland,[2] well I thought that my

1. Charles V, Holy Roman emperor (1519–58), king of Spain (as Charles I, 1516–56).

2. *tierra firme.*

deeds and services would be as illustrious and self-evident as those of my ancestors, and that I would not have any need to speak in order to be counted among those who with complete fidelity and great solicitude administer and carry out the mandates of Your Majesty, and whom you favor. But since neither my counsel[1] nor diligence prevailed in order that the endeavor upon which we were embarked be completed as service to Your Majesty, and since no expedition of as many as have gone to those lands ever saw itself in such grave dangers or had such a wretched and disastrous end as that which God permitted us to suffer on account of our sins, I had no opportunity to perform greater service than this, which is to bring to Your Majesty an account of all that I was able to observe and learn in the nine[a] years that I walked lost and naked through many and very strange lands,[2] as much regarding the locations of the lands and provinces and the distances among them, as with respect to the foodstuffs and animals that are produced in them, and the diverse customs of many and very barbarous peoples with whom I conversed and lived, plus all the other particularities that I could come to know and understand, so that in some manner Your Majesty may be served. Because although the hope that I had of coming out from among them was always very little, my care and effort to remember everything in detail was always very great. This I did so that if at some time our Lord God should wish to bring me to the place where I am now,[3] I would be able to bear witness to my will and serve Your Majesty, inasmuch as the account of it all is, in my opinion, information not trivial for those who in your name might go to conquer those lands and

a. nine] V: ten

1. Cabeza de Vaca here alludes to critical decisions made early in the expedition about which his counsel was disregarded (f7v, f8r–v).

2. Cabeza de Vaca traveled through North American lands for a maximum of eight years—from April 1528, when he arrived with the Narváez expedition on the Florida Peninsula, until he encountered Spaniards in northwestern Mexico in early 1536.

3. Castile.

at the same time bring them[1] to knowledge of the true faith and the true Lord and service to Your Majesty. I wrote all this with such sure knowledge that although some very novel things may be read in it, very difficult for some to believe, they can absolutely give them credence and be assured that I am in everything brief rather than lengthy, and it will suffice for this purpose to have offered it to Your Majesty as such, for which I ask that it be received in the name of service, because this alone is what a man who came away naked could carry out with him.

1. The "barbarous peoples"
referred to above (f2r).

a.] Z: *om.* V: Chapter one: In which is told when the expedition departed and the officials and people who went on it.

b. Suárez] Z: Gutiérrez

[a]On the seventeenth day of the month of June 1527, Governor Pánfilo de Narváez, with the authority and mandate of Your Majesty, departed from the port of Sanlúcar de Barrameda[1] to conquer and govern the provinces that are found from the Río de las Palmas to the cape of *Florida*, which are on the mainland.[2] And the fleet that he led was composed of five ships, in which there went about six hundred men, more or less. Because it is necessary to make mention of them, the officers[3] he commanded were the ones who are named here: Cabeza de Vaca as treasurer and *alguacil mayor*;[4] Alonso Enríquez [as] comptroller; Alonso de Solís[5] as factor of Your Majesty and inspector of mines. A friar of the Order of Saint Francis named Fray Juan Suárez[b] went as commissary,[6] and four other friars of the same order went with him. We arrived at the island of Santo Domingo, where we spent nearly forty-five days stocking up on certain necessary items, notably horses.[7] Here more than one hundred and forty men of our crew deserted us, choosing to remain there because of the favors and promises that the men of that land made to them. We departed from there and arrived at Santiago, which is a port on the island of Cuba, where, during the number of days we were there, the governor resupplied himself with men, arms, and horses. There it occurred that a prominent gentleman

1. The main port of embarkation for the Indies, at the mouth of the Guadalquivir River on the southwestern coast of the Iberian Peninsula.

2. The area referred to here included the lands along the western and northern coast of the Gulf of Mexico from the mouth of the Río Soto la Marina in the present-day state of Tamaulipas in northeastern Mexico to the tip of the Florida Peninsula. In the 1520s the term *Florida* described the vast unexplored lands that lay beyond the northern frontier of New Spain from the Florida Peninsula to the Pacific Coast. Throughout this work, italicized *Florida* is used in contrast to Florida, which denotes the modern-day state.

3. Officials of the royal treasury.

4. Narváez, not Cabeza de Vaca, held royal appointment as

chief law-enforcement official (CDI 16:69, 22:226).

5. Diego de Solís, according to the document assigning him the position of inspector (AGI, Casa de la Contratación 3309, 32-4-29/35, f48v–f51v).

6. Provincial governor in the Order of Saint Francis.

7. Most likely during August and September 1527.

named Vasco Porcallo, resident of the *villa* of Trinidad,[1] which is on the same island, offered to give the governor certain provisions that he possessed in Trinidad, which is located one hundred leagues[2] from the previously mentioned port of Santiago. Taking the entire fleet, the governor departed for there. However, having arrived at a port called Cabo de Santa Cruz,[3] which is located halfway there, it seemed to him that it was a good idea to wait there and send a ship ahead to acquire those provisions. To this end, he ordered a captain [named] Pantoja to go to Trinidad with his ship, and for greater security, he ordered me to go with him. And he [Pánfilo de Narváez] remained with four ships, since on the island of Santo Domingo he had purchased another vessel. Arriving with these two ships at the port of Trinidad, Captain Pantoja went with Vasco Porcallo to the town, which lies one league from the port, to receive the provisions. I remained at sea with the pilots, who told us that we should depart from there as quickly as possible because it was a very bad port and a great number of ships were customarily lost in it. And because what happened to us there was such a notable thing, it seemed to me that to tell it here would not be unrelated to the purpose and goal for which I chose to write an account of this journey. The following morning the weather showed signs of becoming ominous, as it began to rain and the sea became so turbulent that, although I gave permission to those aboard the ship to take to land, many of them, when they saw the inclement weather and that the town was a league away from there, returned to the ship in order to avoid the wet and cold. At this point a canoe arrived from the town,

1. On the southwestern coast of Cuba.

2. A Spanish league was slightly over 3 miles (4.8 kilometers), according to period and modern sources (Covarrubias 757b; Krieger, "Nuevo estudio" 64–68); see Chardon.

3. On the southeastern coast of Cuba, in the region of the Gulf of Guacanayabo.

bringing me a letter from one of its residents, beseeching me to go there and saying that they would give me the provisions that were necessary and available, to which I declined, saying that I could not leave the ships. At midday the canoe returned with another letter in which, insisting greatly, they asked the same thing, and they sent a horse that was to take me. I gave the same reply I had previously given, saying that I would not leave the ships. But the pilots and crew strongly urged me to go so that haste be made and the provisions brought as quickly as possible, so that afterward we could depart from where they had great fear of the ships being lost if they remained there much longer. For this reason I decided to go to the town, although before leaving I made preparations and instructed the pilots that if the south wind, which often causes ships to be lost in that place, came up, and if they found themselves in great danger, they should scuttle the ships and do it in a place where the people and the horses could be saved. And with this I left; although I tried to get some men to go with me in my company, they refused to leave, saying that it was very wet and cold and the town very far away, [and] that the next day, which was Sunday, they would go ashore, with God's help, to hear mass. One hour after I left, the sea became very rough and the north wind was so strong that not even the rowboats dared to leave for shore, nor were the men able in any way to run the ships aground, because the wind was against the prow, such that despite the very great effort against two contrary winds and the heavy rains, they were there that day and Sunday until nightfall. At this time the sea and the storm began to swell so much that there was no less tempest in the town than at sea, because all the houses and churches blew down, and it was necessary for us to band together in groups of seven or eight men, our arms locked with one another, in order to save ourselves from being carried away by the wind. We were as fearful of being killed by walking under the trees as among the houses, since the storm was so great that even the trees, like the houses, fell. In this great storm and continual danger we walked all night without finding an area or place where we could be safe for even half an hour. Walking along in this way we heard all night long, especially after midnight, much noise and a great clamor of voices, and the loud sounds of bells and flutes and tambourines and other instruments, all of which continued until the morning when the storm ceased. In these parts such a fearful thing had never been seen. I prepared a *probanza*[1] documenting it, the testimony of which I sent to Your Majesty.[2] Monday morning we went down to the port and we did not find the ships. There we saw their buoys in the water where we knew they had been lost, and we went along the coast to see if we could find any remains of them. And since we found none, we went into the woods, and walking through them a quarter of a league from the water, we found the rowboat of one of the ships on top of some trees, and ten leagues from there along the coast two men from my ship were found and certain lids of crates, and the bodies were so disfigured from the blows

1. A series of oral testimonies offered by several witnesses, sworn before and written down by a notary public (*escribano*), responding to a questionnaire prepared to establish certain facts.

2. Charles V replied on 27 March 1528 (AGI, Indiferente General 421, 139-1-7) to a 28 November 1527 communication that Cabeza de Vaca had sent to him, which was possibly the *probanza* here mentioned.

of the rocks that they could not be recognized. Also found were a cape and a quilt shredded to ribbons, and not another thing appeared. Sixty men and twenty horses perished in the ships. Those who had gone ashore the day the ships arrived there, probably about thirty persons, were all that remained of the ones there had been on both ships. Thus we found ourselves for some days in great hardship and necessity because the town's provisions and stores had been lost, along with some cattle. The land was left in such a state that it was a great pity to see it: the trees fallen, the woods destroyed, all stripped of leaves and grass. Thus we were there until the fifth of November, when the governor arrived with his four ships, which had also experienced the great tempest and which had escaped by having gotten themselves to a safe place in time. The men he brought in them and the ones he found there were so terrified by what had happened that they greatly feared embarking again in winter, and they begged the governor to spend it there. And he, recognizing their will and that of the residents, wintered there. He put me in charge of the ships and men, so that I would go with them to winter in the port of Jagua,[1] which is twelve leagues from there, where I stayed until the twentieth of February.

[a]At this time the governor arrived there with a brigantine that he had purchased in Trinidad, and he brought with him a pilot named Miruelo; he had taken him because they[b] said that he knew and had been in the Río de las Palmas and was a very good pilot of the entire

a.] Z: *om.* V: Chapter two: How the governor came to the port of Jagua and brought a pilot with him.

b. they] V: he

1. The Bay of Cienfuegos on the southern coast of Cuba.

a. Lixarte] V: Havana

north coast.[1] He also left another ship which he had purchased on the coast of Lixarte,[a] on which Álvaro de la Cerda was stationed as captain, with forty foot soldiers and twelve horsemen. And two days after he arrived, the governor set sail, taking with him four hundred men and eighty horses in four ships and one brigantine. The pilot whom we had recently enlisted guided the ships through the shoals,[2] which they call the shoals of Canarreo, in such a manner that the following day we ran aground.[3] And we were in this predicament for fifteen days, the keels of the ships frequently touching bottom, after which time a storm caused by the south wind brought so much water into the shallows that we were able to get out, although not without great danger. Having departed from here and arriving at Guaniguanico,[c] another storm overtook us and we were nearly shipwrecked. At Cabo de Corrientes we encountered another storm and were there for three days.[4] At the end of them, we rounded Cabo de San Antón and sailed against the wind until we arrived at a point twelve leagues from Havana. And waiting another day to enter the port, a south wind took us and drove us away from land. And we passed over to the coast of *Florida*,[5] and came to land on Tuesday, the twelfth of April,[6] and we went along the coast the way of *Florida*.[7] And on Maundy Thursday we anchored on the same coast at the mouth of a bay, at the back of which we saw certain houses and habitations of Indians.[8]

c. Guaniguanico]
Z: Aguaniguanico

[d]On this same day the comptroller Alonso Enríquez went onto an island in the same bay. And he called to the Indians, who came

d.] Z: *om.* V: Chapter three: How we arrived in *Florida*.

1. Miruelo was most likely "Diego Fernández de Mirnedo [*sic*]," the chief pilot of Francisco de Garay's 1523 expedition from Jamaica to the Río de las Palmas and Pánuco (CDI 26:99).

2. *baxíos.*

3. Off the south coast of Cuba, probably in the Gulf of Batabanó to the east of the Isla de Pinos.

4. On the southwestern tip of Cuba, as the ships sailed around the island's western end.

5. From Ponce de León's discovery of the Florida Peninsula in 1513, *Florida* referred specifically to the peninsula, and more generally to the Spaniards' evolving concept of mainland North America.

6. 12 April 1528 was actually Easter Sunday. The expedition had been at sea for approximately one month.

7. *la vía de la Florida*. Traveling "the way of *Florida*" meant to follow along the coast toward the tip of the Florida Cape. Traveling "the way of Palms" or "the way of Pánuco" signified movement in the opposite direction, toward the mouths of the Río Pánuco and the Río de las Palmas.

8. An inlet slightly north of the mouth of Tampa Bay on Pinellas Peninsula.

and were with him a considerable amount of time, and by means of exchange they gave him fish and some pieces of venison. The following day, which was Good Friday, the governor disembarked with as many people as he could get into the rowboats that the ships carried. And when we arrived at the Indians' *buhíos*,[1] or houses, that we had seen, we found them abandoned and empty because the people had gone away that night in their canoes. One of those *buhíos* was so big that more than three hundred people could fit in it. The others were smaller, and we found a rattle of gold there among the nets. The next day the governor raised the standard on Your Majesty's behalf and took possession of the land in Your royal name and presented his orders and was obeyed as governor just as Your Majesty commanded. In the same manner we presented ours before him, and he obeyed them as required.[2] Then he commanded the rest of the men to disembark and unload the horses that had survived, which were no more than forty-two in number, because the rest of them had perished due to the great storms and long time at sea. And these few that remained were so thin and worn out that for the present we could make little use of them. The next day[3] the Indians from that village came to us. And although they spoke to us, since we did not have an interpreter we did not understand them. But they made many signs and threatening gestures to us and it seemed to us that they were telling us to leave the land, and with this

1. House or habitation in the Taino language of the Caribbean.

2. The formal presentation of orders between the expedition's leader and its officers was a standard requirement on all royally authorized missions.

3. Easter Sunday, 1528, according to Oviedo (583a). This and all subsequent Oviedo citations giving only a page number or page and chapter numbers refer to his account of the Narváez expedition (*Historia* 3:579–618 [bk. 35, chaps. 1–7]).

they parted from us without producing any confrontation and went away.

a.] Z: *om*. V: Chapter four:
How we entered inland.

[a]And the next day the governor decided to go inland to explore the land and see what it contained. The commissary, the inspector of mines, and I went with him, with forty men, and among them six horsemen, whose horses were of little use to us.[1] We followed to the north[2] until, at the hour of vespers, we arrived at a very large bay that seemed to us to go far inland.[3] We remained there that night, and the next day we returned to where the ships and crew were stationed. The governor ordered that the brigantine go along the coast toward *Florida* and look for the port that Miruelo, the pilot, had said he knew.[4] But he had already miscalculated, and he did not know where we were nor where the port was. And the brigantine was ordered, in case it did not find the port, to travel to Havana and pick up Álvaro de la Cerda's ship, and after taking on some provisions, to come to search for us. When the brigantine had departed, the same group of us as before, along with some others, again went inland, and we followed along the coast of the bay we had found and, having gone four leagues, we took four Indians. And we showed them maize to see if they recognized it, because up to that point we had not seen any sign of it. They told us that they would take us to where it could be found. And thus they took us to their village, which is at the back of the bay near there and in which they showed us a little maize that was not yet ready to harvest. There we found many

1. The comptroller, Alonso Enríquez, was serving at this time as Narváez's lieutenant governor (f30v) and remained at the expedition's settlement on the coast (f7r).

2. Northeast (Oviedo 583a).

3. Old Tampa Bay, forming the western arm of Tampa Bay. The Spaniards would name this bay Bahía de la Cruz (f15v).

4. Miruelo claimed to have been acquainted with the mouth of the Río de las Palmas. This place, on the opposite side of the Gulf of Mexico from where the ships had landed, was the original destination of the Narváez expedition.

crates belonging to Castilian merchants, and in each one of them was the body of a dead man, and the bodies were covered with painted deer hides. This seemed to the commissary to be a type of idolatry, and he burned the crates with the bodies in them.[1] We also found pieces of linen cloth and plumes that seemed to be from New Spain. In addition, we found samples of gold. By means of signs we asked the Indians where those things had come from. They indicated to us by gestures that very far away from there there was a province called Apalachen,[c] in which there was much gold, and they made signs to indicate that there were very great quantities of everything we held in esteem.[2] They said that in Palachen[d] there was great bounty. And taking those Indians as guides we departed from there. And going some ten or twelve leagues we found another village of fifteen[3] houses where there was a good-sized plot of sown maize that was ready to be harvested, and we also found some that was[e] dry. And after being there two days, we returned to where the comptroller and the crew and the ships were located, and we told the comptroller and the pilots about what we had seen and the news that the Indians had given us. And the next day, which was the first of May, the governor called aside the commissary, the comptroller, and the inspector, and myself, as well as a sailor named Bartolomé Fernández, and a notary[4] named Jerónimo de Alaniz. And thus all together, he told us that it was his will to enter inland, and that the ships should go along the coast until they arrived at the port,[5] and that the pilots said and believed that going

c. Apalachen] V: Apalache

d. Palachen] V: Apalache

e. was] V: was already

1. Cabeza de Vaca (f66v) later says that these corpses were of Christians. Oviedo (583b) related that Narváez ordered that the crates be burned, and he commented (615a) that the Spaniards learned from the Indians that the corpses were of Christians; he concluded that since these corpses were of Christians they should not have been burned.

2. Oviedo (583b) said that the Indians informed the Spaniards by signs that they had found the crates as well as the woven cloth and other items, apparently from New Spain, in a ship wrecked on that bay.

3. Twelve to fifteen (Oviedo 584a).

4. *escribano.*

5. The mouth of the Río de las Palmas or possibly the settlement of Santisteban del Puerto located south of the mouth of the Río de las Palmas slightly inland on the Río Pánuco.

in the direction of the Río de Palmas they were very close to there. And on this matter he requested that we give him our opinion.[1] I responded that it seemed to me that by no means should he leave the ships without first assuring that they remained in a secure and inhabited port, and that he should take notice that the pilots were not convinced, nor were they all affirming the same thing, nor did they know where they were, and that beyond all this, the horses were in such condition that we could not make use of them in any need that might present itself, and that above all we were traveling mute, that is, without interpreters, through an area where we could hardly make ourselves understood by the Indians or learn about the land what we desired to know, and that we were entering into a land about which we had no information, nor did we know what it was like, nor what was stored in it, nor by what people it was populated, nor in which part of it we were located, and that beyond all this, we did not have adequate provisions to enter a place of which we were ignorant, because having seen the stores of the ships, no more than a pound of hardtack and another of salt pork could be given to each man as a ration[b2] to take in exploring the land, and that in my opinion we should set sail and go to seek a port and a land better for settling, since what we had seen was in itself as unpopulated and as poor as any place that had been discovered in those parts.[3] To the commissary it seemed quite the opposite, he saying that it was not necessary to embark, but rather that, always going along the coast, they should go in search of the port (because the pilots said that going in the direction of Pánuco it would not be but ten or fifteen leagues from there, and that it was not possible, always going along the coast, for us to miss it, because they said that it entered twelve leagues inland),[4] and that the first ones to find it should wait there for the others, and that

b. man as a ration] Z: man of reason

1. *parecer.* Formal opinion recorded and certified by the notary.

2. *hombre de ración.* The Zamora (1542) edition uses *razón* (reason) in place of *ración* (ration), so that the original text might have been read, "to each man of reason."

3. Oviedo (584a) adds that Cabeza de Vaca also argued that Narváez should wait for the return of Miruelo in the brigantine with Álvaro de la Cerda's ship and provisions

from Havana before initiating an overland journey.

4. The search for the Río de las Palmas, and perhaps also Santisteban del Puerto on the Río Pánuco, determined the route of travel directly along the coast or slightly inland and parallel to it. The entire expedition would follow this course west along the coast of the Gulf of Mexico, and the final four survivors would seemingly unintentionally abandon it in 1535 (see f47v–f48r).

a. the] V: the other

b. the others] V: *om.*

c. he] Z: they

to embark was to tempt God, because since we departed from Castile we had suffered so many hardships and had experienced so many storms, so many losses of ships and men until arriving there, and that for these reasons he should go along the coast until reaching the port and that the[a] ships with the other men should go along the same route until arriving at the same port. To all the others[b] who were there assembled it seemed appropriate to do this in this manner, except for the notary,[1] who said that, rather than abandoning the ships, they should be left in a known and secure port and in an area that was inhabited; that once this was done, he [the governor] could enter inland and do whatever seemed best to him. The governor followed his opinion as well as what the others counseled him. I, having seen his resolution, requested on behalf of Your Majesty that he[c] not leave the ships without their being in port and secure, and thus I asked that my request be certified by the notary we had there with us.[2] He [the governor] responded that since he agreed with the assessment of the majority of the other officials and the commissary, I had no right to make these demands of him. And he asked the notary to certify that on account of there not being adequate foodstuffs in that land to establish a settlement or a port for the ships, he was moving the settlement that he had established there and was going with it in search of the port and of land that would be better. And then he commanded that the people who were going to go with him be advised to supply themselves with whatever was necessary for the journey. And when this was done, in the presence of those who were there he said to me that since I objected so much and feared the inland expedition, I should stay and take charge of the ships

---

1. Jerónimo de Alaniz (f7r).

2. These certification procedures formed part of the juridical protocols by which formal actions were taken and documented on Spanish expeditions of conquest.

and the people who remained on them and set up a camp if I arrived before him. I refused to do this. And after having gone from there that same afternoon, saying that it did not seem to him that he could entrust it to anyone else, he sent me a messenger to say that he was beseeching me to take charge of it. And he, seeing that in spite of entreating me so much I still declined to accept it, asked me why I avoided doing so, to which I responded that I refused to take that responsibility because I was certain and knew that he would not see the ships again nor the ships him, and that I understood this on seeing how unprepared they were to go inland, and that I was more willing than he and the others to expose myself to danger and endure whatever he and the others were to endure than to take charge of the ships and give occasion that it be said, as I had opposed the overland expedition, that I remained out of fear, for which my honor would be under attack, and that I preferred risking my life to placing my honor in jeopardy. He, seeing that he could not prevail upon me, beseeched many others to speak with me about it and beg me to do it, to whom I responded the same as I had to him. And thus, through his lieutenant,[1] he dispatched an order by which an *alcalde*[2] he brought with him, named Caravallo, was to remain with the ships.

b.] Z: *om.* V: Chapter five: How the governor left the ships.

[b]Saturday, the first of May,[3] the same day that this had happened, he [the governor] commanded that each one of those who was to go with him be given two pounds[4] of hardtack and half a pound of salt pork. And thus we set out to enter inland.[5] We took with us a total of three hundred men. Among them went the commissary, Fray

1. Evidently the comptroller, Alonso Enríquez.

2. Magistrate, first-instance judge.

3. 1 May 1528 was actually a Friday.

4. One pound (Oviedo 584b).

5. Cabeza de Vaca omits telling here about the loss of a ship and other events that occurred prior to his departure. He relates this information, as well as the account of what happened to the other three ships, the brigantine, and the ship brought by Álvaro de la Cerda, at the end of the narrative (f65v–f66v). Unlike the shipwreck, these other events occurred subsequent to his departure, and he did not learn about them until he arrived in New Spain and Castile eight and nine years later, in 1536 and 1537, respectively.

a. Suárez] Z: Xuárez

Juan Suárez,[a] and another friar, who was called Fray Juan de Palos, and three clerics,[1] and the [royal] officials. We the horsemen who went with them numbered forty. And thus we traveled with those provisions, which we carried for fifteen days without finding anything to eat other than hearts of palm of the type found in Andalusia. During this entire time we did not find a single Indian, nor did we see a single house or village. And at the end [of the fifteen days] we came to a river[2] that we crossed by swimming and on rafts with very great difficulty. It took us an entire day to cross it because it had a very strong current. Having crossed to the other side, nearly two hundred Indians, more or less, confronted us. The governor went out to them, and after having spoken to them by means of signs, they gestured to us in such a way that we had to turn on them. And we captured five or six of them, and these Indians took us to their houses, which were a half league from there, where we found great quantities of maize ready to be harvested. And we gave infinite thanks to our Lord for having aided us in so great a need, because since we were most certainly new to these hardships, beyond the fatigue we suffered, we came very worn out from hunger. And on the third day after having arrived there, we—the comptroller, the inspector, the commissary, and I—met together, and we begged the governor to send scouts to look for the sea to see if we could find a port, because the Indians said that the sea was not very far from there. He replied to us that we should not trouble ourselves with talking about that, because it was very far from there. And since I was the one who importuned him the most, he told me that I should go

1. *clérigos.* Identified earlier (f3r) as Franciscan friars.
2. Withlacoochee River.

to find it and seek a port, and that I was to go on foot with forty men to do this. And thus the next day I departed with Captain Alonso del Castillo and forty men of his company. And thus we walked until noon, when we arrived at some sandbars of the sea that seemed to extend far inland. We walked through them about a league and a half[1] in water up to our knees, treading on oyster shells from which we received many cuts on our feet and that were the cause of much difficulty for us, until we arrived at the river that we had first crossed, which passed through that same bay. And since we could not cross it because we were so ill equipped for the purpose, we returned to camp and told the governor what we had found, and how it was necessary to cross the river again in the same place where we first had crossed it[2] in order to explore that bay well and see if there was a port there. And the next day he ordered a captain named Valenzuela to cross the river with sixty[3] foot soldiers and six horsemen, and to follow the river downstream until arriving at the sea, and to look for a port;[4] and after having been there two days, he returned. And he said that he had found the bay, and that all of it was shallow with water only knee-deep, and that a port could not be found, and that he had seen five or six canoes of Indians that crossed from one side to the other, and that they wore many plumes. Having learned this, the next day we departed from there, always going in pursuit of that province of Apalachen[c] that the Indians had told us about, taking as guides the ones from among them whom

c. Apalachen] V: Apalache

1. Two leagues (Oviedo 585a).

2. See (f9r).

3. Forty (Oviedo 585a).

4. The Spaniards evidently believed that this river, which emptied into the Gulf of Mexico on the west coast of the Florida Peninsula, was potentially the Río de las Palmas or the Río Pánuco, and that they would find their ships at the mouth of it.

we had captured.[1] And thus we walked until the seventeenth of June, during which time we found no Indians who dared to face us. And there, a native lord,[2] carried on the shoulders of an Indian and covered with a painted deer hide, came forth to meet us. He brought with him many people, and before him they came playing reed flutes. And thus he arrived to where the governor was and he spent an hour with him. And by gestures we gave him to understand that we were going to Palachen,[b] and by those which he made, it seemed to us that he was an enemy of the people of Apalachen,[c] and that he would go to help us against them. We gave him beads and bells[3] and other items of exchange, and he gave the governor the deerskin garment he was wearing, and thus he returned. And we went following him in the direction that he took. That night we reached a river that was very deep and very wide and had a very strong current.[4] And because we did not dare to cross it with rafts, we made a canoe for the purpose, and it took us a day to cross it. And if the Indians had wanted to attack us, they could easily have obstructed our passage, and even with their help we had great difficulty. One of the horsemen, who was named Juan Velázquez, a native of Cuéllar, because he did not want to wait, went into the river on his horse,[d] and the current, since it was strong, swept him off his horse, and he held tight to the reins, and thus he drowned and drowned the horse as well. And those Indians of that lord, who was called Dulchanchellin, found the horse and told us where we could find him [Velázquez] downstream, and thus they went to retrieve him. And his death gave us much grief, because up to that point none of us had perished.[5] The horse fed many that night. Once departed from there, we arrived the next day at the village of that lord, and there he sent us maize. That

b. Palachen] V: Apalache
c. Apalachen] V: Apalache
d. on his horse] V: *om.*

1. The account that follows, through the expedition's arrival at Apalache (f10v), is absent from Oviedo's account.

2. Dulchanchellin, as Cabeza de Vaca notes below. Cabeza de Vaca used the Spanish "señor" as well as the Taino "cacique" to refer to native rulers.

3. *caxcaveles.* Covarrubias (315a) observed that such metal bells were used to decorate horses on festive occasions and served as warning devices in general. He noted their use by musicians and as a way to track hunting birds and stock animals such as mules.

4. Suwannee River.

5. Velázquez was the first to die from among those who had gone on the overland expedition in *Florida*; sixty men had been killed in the hurricane in Cuba (see f5r).

night, where they went to get water, they shot at one of our Christians, and God willed that they not wound him. The next day we left from there without even one of the Indians of that area appearing, because all of them had fled. But following our course, there appeared Indians who came prepared for war. And although we called to them, they refused to return or even hold their ground, but, rather, they retreated, following us along the same road we were traveling. The governor left some of the horsemen behind as an ambush on the road, so that as the Indians passed, they assaulted them and took three or four Indians. And we took these Indians as guides from that point onward; they took us through land very difficult to maneuver and glorious to see, because in it there are very great forests, and the trees wonderfully tall, and there are so many that are fallen upon the ground that they hindered our progress, so that we could not pass without making many detours and having very great difficulty. Of those trees that were not downed, many were split from top to bottom by lightning bolts that strike in that land where there are always great storms and tempests. With these difficulties we walked until the day after the Day of Saint John,[1] when we arrived within sight of Apalachen[b] without being perceived by the Indians of the area.[2] We gave many thanks to God upon seeing ourselves so near it (believing that what they had told us about that land was true, that there the great hardships that we had suffered would end), as much because of the long and difficult road we had walked, as because of the great hunger we had suffered. Because although sometimes we found

b. Apalachen] V: Apalache

1. 25 June, following the saint's day of 24 June.

2. Somewhere in the region between the Aucilla and Apalachicola Rivers in the north-central portion of the present-day state of Florida.

maize, most of the time we walked seven or eight leagues without finding any.[1] And there were many among us who, apart from the great fatigue and hunger they suffered and, since there was no other recourse, had wounds on their backs from carrying their weapons on their shoulders. But on finding ourselves where we desired to be, and where they told us there were so many foodstuffs and so much gold, it seemed to us that a great portion of our hardship and weariness had been lifted from us.

c.] Z: *om.* V: Chapter six: How we arrived at Apalache.

d. Apalachen] V: Apalache

[c]Upon arriving within sight of Apalachen,[d] the governor ordered that I take nine horsemen and fifty foot soldiers and enter the village. And thus the inspector[2] and I attacked it. And having entered it, we found only women and children, since at that time the men were not in the village. But a little while later, as we walked through it, they rushed in and began to attack, shooting us with arrows. And they killed the inspector's horse, but in the end they fled and left us alone. There we found a great quantity of maize that was ready to be harvested, as well as much that they had dried and stored. We found many deer hides and among them some small woven mantles of poor quality with which the women partially cover their bodies. They had many vessels for grinding maize. In the village there were forty small houses, built low to the ground and in protected places, out of fear of the great tempests that commonly occur with great frequency in that land. The construction is of grass. And they are surrounded by very thick woods and great groves and many lagoons where there are many and very large fallen trees that form obstructions

1. Oviedo (585a) claimed the expedition sometimes went four or five days without finding maize.

2. Alonso (Diego) de Solís.

a.] Z: *om.* V: Chapter seven:
Of the character of the land.

b. Apalachen] V: Apalache

e. Apalachen] V: Apalache

f. are] V: are so

and make it impossible to traverse the land without great difficulty and danger.

[a]For the most part, the land from where we disembarked up to this village and province of Apalachen[b] is flat, the ground being composed of hard, firm sand. Throughout the entire land there are very large trees and open woods where there are walnut trees, and laurels and others that are called liquidambars, cedars, savins and evergreen oaks and pines and oaks, [and] palmettos of the type commonly found in Castile. Throughout, there are many large and small lagoons, some very difficult to traverse, in part because of their great depth, in part because of the many downed trees in them. Their floors are of sand, and those we found in the district of Apalachen[e] are larger than those we had found previously. There are many fields of maize in this province. And the houses are[f] scattered about the countryside in the same manner as those of the Gelves.[1] The animals that we saw in it are deer of three types, rabbits and hares, bears and lions, and other wild beasts, among which we saw an animal that carries its young in a pouch in its belly, and all the while the offspring are small, they carry them there until they know how to forage for food, and if by chance they are searching for food and human beings come upon them, the mother does not flee until she has gathered them up in her pouch.[2] In that region it is very cold. There are many good pastures for grazing cattle. There are birds of many types: geese in great numbers, ducks, mallards, royal-ducks, fly-catchers and night-herons and herons, [and] partridges. We saw many falcons, gyrfalcons, sparrow hawks, merlins, and many other birds.

1. The island of Djerba, located off southeastern Tunisia in the Mediterranean at the entrance to the Gulf of Gabes.

2. The common opossum (*Didelphis virginiana*), the only species of opossum native to North America.

Two days[a] after we arrived in Apalachen,[b] the Indians who had fled from there came to us in peace, asking us for their women and children. And we gave them to them, except that the governor kept with him a cacique of theirs, which was the cause of their being greatly offended. And later, the next day, they returned to make war. And they attacked us with so much skill and swiftness that they successfully set fire to the houses in which we were lodged.[1] But as we came out, they fled and took to the lagoons that were nearby. And because of this and the great fields of maize in the area, we could not do them any harm except to one whom we killed. The following day other Indians from another village on the other side came to us and attacked us in the same manner as the first ones had done. And in the same way they escaped, save one of them who also died. We were in this village for twenty-five days,[2] during which time we made three incursions into the land, and we found it very sparsely inhabited and very difficult to traverse

because of the very[e] difficult passes and woods and lagoons it contained. We asked the cacique whom we had detained from them and the other Indians whom we brought along with us who were neighbors and enemies of theirs about the character and habitation of the land and the quality of the people and about the food supply and everything else in it. They told us, each one

by himself, that the largest village of that entire land was Apalachen,[f] and that ahead there were fewer people, who were much poorer than they, and that the land was poorly populated and its inhabitants widely dispersed, and that going forward there were great lagoons and dense woods and great empty and unpopulated areas. We asked them later about the land that lay to the south, what villages and what provisions it contained. They said

1. According to Oviedo (585b), some two hundred Indians attacked the village.

2. Twenty-six (Oviedo 585b).

c. and that there] V: *om.*

f. Tescuco] Z: Tezaico

that through that land, going to the sea was a nine-day journey, and that there,ᶜ there was a village called Aute,¹ and the Indians of that place had a great deal of maize and they had frijoles and squash, and that because of being so close to the sea they obtained fish, and that these people were their friends. Seeing the poverty of the land and the unfavorable reports that they gave us about the population and everything else, and since the Indians made war on us continually, wounding the people and the horses when we were at the places where we went to get water (and doing this from the lagoons and so safely that we could do them no harm, because they shot arrows at us while being submerged in them) and had killed a lord of Tescucoᶠ² who was called Don Pedro, whom the commissary had brought with him, we decided to depart from there and go to seek the sea and that village of Aute about which they had told us. And thus we departed after having been there for twenty-five days.³ The first day we crossed those lagoons and passes without seeing a single Indian. But on the second day we came to a lagoon very difficult to traverse because the water was chest-high and in it there were many fallen trees. When we were in the middle of it, many Indians, who were hidden behind the trees so that we could not see them, attacked us; others were on top of the logs. And they began to shoot arrows at us in such a way that they wounded many of our men and horses, and they captured the guide we carried with us before we could get out of the lagoon. And after getting out of it, they again pursued us, trying to block our path, so that it did us no good to get out of it, nor to increase our

1. In the region between the Aucilla and Apalachicola Rivers.

2. Kingdom to the east of Tenochtitlán whose warriors served as Cortés's allies in the conquest of Mexico (1519–21) and continued in the service of the Spaniards in further conquest efforts.

3. Twenty-six (Oviedo 586a). The expedition remained at Apalache from about 25 June to 19–20 July 1528.

strength and ardor to fight against them, because they went back into the lagoon and from there they wounded our people and horses. Seeing this, the governor ordered that the horsemen dismount and attack them on foot. The comptroller dismounted with them and thus they attacked them, and all retreated into a lagoon, and in this manner we won the passage from them. In this struggle there were some of our wounded who could not make use of the good weapons they carried, and there were men this day who swore that they had seen two oaks, each one of them as thick as a man's lower leg, pierced through and through by the arrows of the Indians, and this is not to be wondered at, having seen the strength and skill with which they shoot them, because I myself saw an arrow in the base of a poplar tree that had entered it to the depth of a *xeme*.[1] All the Indians we had seen from *Florida* to here[2] are archers, and as they are of[c] large build and go about naked, from a distance they appear to be giants. They are a people wonderfully well built,[3] very lean and of great strength and agility. The bows they use are as thick as an arm [and] eleven or twelve spans[4] long so that they can shoot arrows at two hundred paces with such great skill that they never miss their target. After having departed from the point of this crossing, a league's distance from there we arrived at another [lagoon] of the same type, except that this one was much worse on account of it being so long, extending for half a league. We passed this one freely and without being hindered by Indians, who, since in the first skirmish they had spent all the ammunition of arrows they had, had been left without anything with which to venture to attack us. Making a similar crossing the following day, I found the track of people ahead of us, and I notified the governor, who was traveling with the

c. of] V: of such

1. The distance between the tip of the thumb and the tip of the outstretched index finger (Covarrubias 1015a; DRAE 768b).

2. Roughly, the lands adjacent to the northern half of the west coast of the Florida Peninsula.

3. *bien dispuesta*. Of well-proportioned physical stature, or of good personal disposition, inclinations, or intentions (Covarrubias 477b; DRAE 486b, 1238c). Cabeza de Vaca frequently makes reference to the former (see also f17r, f24r, f32r, f47r, f53r), occasionally to the latter (f18v, f47v, f52v, f60r).

4. Equivalent to the English span, *palmo* refers to the distance between the tip of the thumb and the little finger of a spread hand (Covarrubias 847a; DRAE 965a; *Webster's Ninth* 1130a).

rear guard. And thus although the Indians charged us, since we went forewarned, they were unable to do us any harm. And having come out into the clearing, they continued to follow us. We doubled back on them on two sides and killed two of their Indians, and they wounded me and two or three other Christians. And because they took refuge from us in the woods, we could do them no more ill or harm. In this way we traveled for eight days. And from this passage about which I have told, no more Indians confronted us until one league ahead, which is the place to which I have said we were going.[1] There, as we were making our way ahead, Indians came out, and without being perceived they attacked the rear guard. And at the shouts of a boy of an hidalgo[2] of those who were going along there, named Avellaneda, this Avellaneda turned back and went to rescue them. And the Indians struck him with an arrow at the edge of his breastplate, and the wound was such that almost the entire arrow passed through his neck, and later he died there, and we carried his body to Aute. We arrived there after nine days' travel from Apalachen.[b] And when we arrived, we found all the people of the village gone and the houses burned, and much maize[3] and squash and frijoles that were all on the point of being ready for harvest. We rested there for two days, and when these had passed, the governor beseeched me to go look for the sea, because the Indians said that it was very near there; along this route we had already discovered it by means of a very great river that we found on this path, which we had named the Río de la Magdalena.[c4] Seeing this, the following day I left to explore it together with the commissary and Captain Castillo and Andrés Dorantes as well as seven[5] other horsemen and fifty foot soldiers. And we marched

b. Apalachen] V: Apalache

c. Magdalena] Z: Madalena

1. Aute.

2. The boy was probably a native youth in the Spaniard's service, who, as an hidalgo, was a member of the lower-ranking nobility of Castile.

3. According to Oviedo (587a), the fields of maize had also been burned.

4. Probably a river that flows into Apalachee Bay (e.g., Aucilla, Saint Marks, Ochlockonee). Cabeza de Vaca seems to suggest that this river had earlier been followed to the sea, evidently in search of a port and the expedition's ships.

5. Oviedo (587a) claimed there were nine horsemen and did not mention the commissary.

until the hour of vespers, when we arrived at a bay or entrance to the sea where we found many oysters which pleased the men very much, and we gave many thanks to God for having brought us there. The next morning I sent twenty men to reconnoiter the coast and to take note of its layout; they returned during the night of the following day, saying that those coves and bays were very large and went so far inland that they made it very difficult to find what we were looking for and that the seacoast was very far from there. Informed of this news and having seen the poor situation and means there were for reaching the coast through that area, I returned to the governor. And when we arrived, we found him ill, along with many others. And the previous night the Indians had attacked them and put them in exceedingly great danger on account of the sickness that had overcome them. They had also killed a horse. I gave an account to the governor[c] of what I had done and the poor lay of the land. That day we remained there.

[d]The following day we departed from Aute and marched the whole day until we arrived to where I had been.[1] The journey was difficult in the extreme, because neither the horses were sufficient to carry all the sick, nor did we know what remedy to seek because every day they languished, which was a spectacle of very great sorrow and pain to see the necessity and hardship in which we found ourselves. Having arrived and seen the little prospect there was for going forward, because there was no way that would allow us to proceed, and even if there had been, the men could [not] have gone on because most of them were ill and in such a state that there were few by whom any progress could have been made. I refrain here from telling this at greater length because each one can imagine for himself what could happen in a land so strange

c. to the governor] V: *om.*

d.] Z: *om.* V: Chapter eight: How we departed from Aute.

1. At a saltwater bay, well inland from the open seacoast in the vicinity of Apalachee Bay.

and so poor and so lacking in every single thing that it seemed impossible either to be in it or to escape from it. But since the most certain remedy is God our Lord and in him our faith never falters, another thing occurred that worsened the situation more than all of this; that is, among the horsemen, the majority of them began to plan secretly to find relief for themselves and abandon the governor and the sick men, who were altogether powerless, without strength or the means to impose authority. But since among them there were many hidalgos and men of good breeding, they refused to let this happen without informing the governor and the officials of Your Majesty. And since we discredited their intentions and placed before them the occasion on which they were abandoning their captain and those who were sick and without strength, and above all else removing themselves from the service of Your Majesty, they agreed to remain, affirming that what would be the fate of one would be the fate of all without any one abandoning the others. This being understood by the governor, he called everyone to him and each one by himself, soliciting opinions about so poor a land in order to be able to leave it and seek some solution, since there there was none, a full third of the men being gravely ill and the number of them increasing by the hour, such that we held it to be certain that we would all be thus, from which nothing could follow but death, which on account of being in such a place was to us all the more ominous. And having considered these and many other obstacles, and having tried many solutions, we decided upon one very difficult to put into effect, which was to build ships in which we could leave. To everyone it seemed impossible, because we did not know how to make them nor were there tools, nor iron, nor a forge, nor oakum, nor pitch, nor ropes, nor finally any single thing of all those that are necessary, nor was there anyone who knew anything about carrying this out, and above all there was nothing to eat while they were being constructed, nor were there adequate men to perform the tasks we had mentioned. And considering all this, we agreed to think about it for a while longer, and the conversation ceased for that day, and each one went off, entrusting himself to our Lord God to direct him where he might be best served. The next day God ordained that a member of the company came, saying that he would make some tubes of wood, and with some deerskins some bellows would be made. And since we were in such straits that anything that had some semblance of a solution seemed to us a good thing, we said that he should set to the task. And we agreed to make the nails and saws and axes and other tools of which there was such great necessity from the stirrups and spurs and crossbows and other iron objects that we had. And we determined that, in order to provide means of sustenance during the period in which this was to be carried out, four incursions would be made into Aute with all the horses and people well enough to take part, and that every third day a horse would be killed to be distributed among those who were working on building the ships and those who were sick. The forays were made with all the available men and horses, and in them up to four hundred *fanegas*[1] of maize were seized, although not without fights and skirmishes with the Indians. We had many palmettos gathered in order to make use of their fibers and coverings, twisting and preparing them to use

1. A measure commonly used for grain (Covarrubias 584b), equivalent to about 1.6 bushels in Spain (Hemming 518). Approximately 640 bushels of maize were seized from the Indians at Aute.

in place of oakum for the rafts, the construction of which was begun by the only carpenter[1] in the company. And we put so much effort into it that, beginning them on the fourth day of August, five rafts of twenty-two cubits[2] each were finished on the twentieth day of September, caulked with the oakum made from the palmettos, and we tarred them with a certain pitch that a Greek named Don Teodoro[3] extracted from some pine trees. And from the same covering of the palmettos and from the tails and manes of the horses, we made cords and ropes, and from our shirts we made sails. And from the savins growing there we made the oars that it seemed to us were necessary. And such was the land in which our sins had placed us, that only with very great effort could we find stones for ballast[b] on the rafts, because in all that area we had not seen even one. We also stripped the legs of the horses whole and cured their hides in order to make vessels in which to carry water. During this time, some went about gathering shellfish in the inlets and coves of the sea, and on the two occasions on which the Indians attacked them, they killed ten of our men within sight of camp without our being able to rescue them; we found them shot through and through with arrows, and although some of them had good weapons, their arms were not sufficient to prevent this from happening because the Indians shot arrows with as much skill and force as I have described above.[4] And upon the declaration and oath of our pilots, from the bay that we named the Bay of the Cross[5] to this point, we had traveled two hundred and eighty leagues, more or

b. ballast] V: ballast and anchors

1. Apparently the Portuguese Álvaro Fernández (f23v).

2. *codo.* One of several possible Spanish units of measure: *codo a la mano, codo real, codo geométrico* (Covarrubias 332a). The cubit is any of various ancient units of length based on the length of the forearm to the tip of the middle finger and equivalent to approximately 18–21 inches (46–53 centimeters) (*Webster's Ninth* 313b). One estimate of the size of the raft would be approximately 33 feet (10 meters) in length.

3. This Greek will reappear later in the narrative (f18r), left among the native groups on the coast somewhere between the western part of the panhandle of modern-day Florida and the mouth of the Mississippi River.

4. See (f13r).

5. Old Tampa Bay (f6v).

a. another] V: *om.*

less.[1] In all this land we saw no mountains nor any sign of them. And before we embarked, more than another[a] forty men, excluding the ones whom the Indians had killed, died of sickness and starvation. On the twenty-second day of the month of September all but the last horse had been eaten. And this day we embarked in this order: the governor's raft carried forty-nine men; as many men went on the one he assigned to the comptroller and the commissary; he gave the third one to Captain Alonso del Castillo

c. other] V: *om.*

and Andrés Dorantes with forty-eight men; he gave another to two other[c] captains named Téllez and Peñalosa with forty-seven men; the last one he assigned to the inspector and me with forty-nine men.[2] And after loading the provisions and clothing, the rafts rode so low that only a *xeme*[3] of their sides showed above water, and in addition to this, we were so crowded that we could not even move. And so greatly can necessity prevail that it made us risk going in this manner and placing ourselves in a sea so treacherous, and without any one of us who went having any knowledge of the art of navigation.

e.] Z: *om.* V: Chapter nine: How we departed from the Bay of Horses.

[e]That bay from which we departed is called the Bay of Horses.[4] And we went for seven days through those inlets in water no more than waist deep, without finding any sign of the coast, and at the end of them we arrived at an island that was near the shore.[5] My raft went ahead, and from it we saw five canoes of Indians approaching, which

---

1. Probably only one third of this distance had been covered. From 1519 the length of the northern coast of the Gulf of Mexico between Pánuco and the tip of the Florida Peninsula had been estimated to be three hundred leagues.

2. Of the approximately three hundred men who left the ships on the expedition on 1 May 1528 near Old Tampa Bay, more than fifty apparently perished on the overland trek. Cabeza de Vaca here accounts for 242 if the leaders of the rafts are included in the numbers cited. Oviedo (588ab) accounted for 239.

3. See (f13r).

4. Some point along the coast in Apalachee Bay.

5. The expedition seems to have wandered through shallow inland waterways for seven days before coming to the open water of the sea. The island is not identifiable, since the Spaniards' location in the region of Apalachee Bay cannot be determined.

they abandoned and left in our hands, seeing that we were headed for them. The other rafts went ahead and came upon some houses on the same island where we found much mullet and dried roe, which were of great help for the necessity in which we found ourselves. After taking them, we went ahead, and two leagues from there we crossed a strait that the island makes with the mainland and we named it Saint Michael, having come upon it on that saint's day.[1] And having departed, we arrived on the coast where, with the five canoes that I had taken from the Indians, we partially repaired the rafts, making washboards out of the canoes and adding them so that the sides of the rafts protruded two spans[2] above water. This done, we again took up our journey along the coast in the direction of the Río de Palmas, each day our hunger and thirst increasing, because the provisions were very few and nearly exhausted and our water was gone because the vessels that we had made from the legs of the horses later rotted and were of no use whatsoever. And furthermore, sometimes we entered inlets and bays that extended far inland; we found all of them shallow and dangerous. And thus we went through them for thirty days, during which time we sometimes found Indian fishermen, people poor and wretched. At the end of these thirty days, at which time our need for water was extreme, going near the coast one night we detected a canoe approaching. And having seen it, we waited for it to arrive. And it refused to present itself. And although we called to it, it refused to return or wait for us. And since it was nighttime we did not follow it, and we went on our way. When

1. 29 September 1528. Cabeza de Vaca's geographic references to places the expedition visited on their raft journey from the Bay of Horses to the Texas coast (22 September 1528 to November 1528) cannot be identified with certainty.

2. See (f13r).

dawn came we saw a small island. And we went to it to see if we could find water, but our efforts were in vain, because there was none. Being thus anchored, a great storm overtook us, causing us to remain there for six[1] days without daring to take to the sea. And as it had been five days since we had drunk any water, our thirst was so great that we were obliged to drink salt water. And some were so careless in doing so that suddenly five[2] men died on us. I tell this briefly in this manner because I do not think there is need to tell in detail the miseries and hardships in which we found ourselves, since considering the place where we were and the little hope we had of survival, each one can imagine a great deal of what would happen there. And as we saw our thirst increasing and the water killing us, even though the storm had not ceased we agreed to entrust ourselves to God our Lord and risk the danger of the sea, rather than await the certainty of death that our thirst foreboded. And thus we departed, taking the route of the canoe we had seen the night that we had come through there. And on this day we found ourselves many times sinking and so lost that there was not one among us who did not take death to be a certainty. It pleased God, who at the time of greatest need customarily shows his favor, that at sunset we rounded a point that the land makes, where we found great calm and refuge. Many canoes came out to meet us and the Indians who came in them spoke to us and, without wanting to wait for us, turned back. They were large people and well proportioned and they did not carry bows or arrows. We

1. Three (Oviedo 588b).
2. Five or six (Oviedo 588b).

went following them to their houses, which were near there at the edge of the water, and we went ashore. And in front of the houses we found many vessels of water and a great quantity of cooked fish. And the lord of those lands offered all that sustenance to the governor, and taking it with him, he took him to his house. The houses of these people were made of woven rushes and appeared to be stationary. And after we entered the cacique's house, he gave us much fish. And we gave him some of the maize that we carried, and they ate it in our presence and they asked us for more and we gave it to them. And the governor gave him many trinkets whereupon, being with the cacique in his house in the middle of the night, the Indians suddenly attacked us, as well as those who were very sick, lying scattered on the shore.[1] And they also assaulted the house of the cacique where the governor was, and they wounded him in the face with a rock. Those who were there captured the cacique, but since his people were so near, they released him, and he left in their hands a cloak of sable skins that I believe are the finest to be found anywhere in the world. And they have a scent that resembles nothing other than ambergris and musk, and it is so strong that it can be detected at a great distance. We saw other furs there, but none like these. Those of us who were there, seeing the governor wounded, put him on the raft and we made all the rest of the men return to the rafts with him. And about fifty of us remained on land to fight against the Indians, who attacked us three times that night and did so with such force that each time they made us retreat more than

1. Oviedo (589a) states that three of the Spaniards were killed here.

the distance of a stone's throw. Not one of us remained uninjured and I was wounded in the face, and if, as very few arrows could be found, the Indians had been better provided with them, they undoubtedly would have done us great harm. The last time, Captains Dorantes and Peñalosa and Téllez hid themselves with fifteen men in ambush. And they attacked them from behind and in that way made them flee and leave us. The next morning I broke up more than thirty of their canoes, which were of use to us against the cold of a north wind, since we had to be there the entire day, being very cold, without daring to enter the sea because of the great storm that was upon it. This having passed, we embarked again and sailed for three[1] days. And since we had brought little water, and the vessels that we had to carry it likewise were very few, we again found ourselves in this first of all necessities. And continuing our course, we entered an estuary, and while there, we saw a canoe of Indians approaching. Upon calling to them they came to us. And the governor, to whose raft they had arrived, asked them for water, and they offered to bring it provided that we give them something in which to carry it. And a Greek Christian named Doroteo Teodoro, of whom mention was made earlier,[2] said that he wanted to go with them. The governor and others tried very hard to prevent him from going, but they were unable, since in any case he wanted to go with them. And so he left, and he took a black man[3] with him. And the Indians left as hostages two of their company. And at night the Indians returned and brought our vessels without water, and they did not bring the Christians whom they had taken. And those they had left as hostages, with the encouragement of those who called to them, tried to throw themselves into the water.

1. Three or four (Oviedo 589a).

2. See (f15v).

3. *un negro.* An African slave on the expedition, described a few lines below and on (f18v) as a Christian. African slaves were brought to the Indies from at least 1501, when royal instructions to Nicolás de Ovando as governor of its islands and mainland required that they be Christian, that is, born in the possession of Christians under Castilian rule (CDI 31:23).

But those who were on the raft stopped them, and thus the Indians in the canoe went fleeing. And they left us very perplexed and saddened at having lost those two Christians.

b.] Z: *om*. V: Chapter ten: Of the skirmish we had with the Indians.

[b]When morning came, many canoes of Indians approached us, asking us for their two companions who had remained on the raft as hostages. The governor said that he would release them provided that they bring the two Christians they had carried off. With these people came five or six[1] lords, and they seemed to us to be the most well disposed people and of the greatest authority and bearing of any we had seen up to that point, even though they were not as large as the others of whom we have spoken. They wore their hair loose and very long, and they were covered with cloaks of sable skins like the one we had previously taken, and some of them were made in a very strange manner, because they were laced together with ties of tawny-colored leather that made them very handsome. They begged us to go with them, claiming that they would give us the Christians and water and many other things. And during this time many canoes were coming toward us, trying to close the mouth of the estuary. And therefore because of this, since this was a very dangerous land to enter, we went out to sea, where we were surrounded by them until midday. And since they refused to return the Christians to us, and for this reason we would not give them the Indian hostages, they began to hurl stones at us with slings and throw spears, feigning to shoot arrows at us, although among all of them we saw no more than three or four bows.

1. Three or four (Oviedo 589b).

Being in this dispute the wind came up, and they turned back and left us. And thus we sailed that day[1] until the hour of vespers, when my raft, which was leading the way, came upon a point that the land made and on the opposite side a very large river could be seen.[2] And on an island that the point made I ordered that we anchor in order to wait for the other rafts. The governor refused to come, and instead entered a bay very near there, in which there were many islands. And there we came together, and from the sea we drank fresh water, because the river entered the sea as a freshet. And in order to toast some of the maize that we carried, because we had been eating it raw for two days, we disembarked on that island, but since we found no firewood, we agreed to go to the river that was behind the point one league from there. On going, the current was so great that it was not possible to land; instead it drove us away from the shore. And while we were working and struggling to reach land, the north wind, which was blowing from the land, became so strong that it drove us out to sea without our being able to do anything about it. And half a league out to sea, at the point to which we had been driven, we took a sounding, and we found that even with thirty fathoms[3] we could not touch bottom, and we could not determine whether the current was the reason we were unable to do so. And thus we sailed two[4] days, still struggling to reach land, and at the end of them, a little before sunrise we saw many spires of smoke along the coast. And endeavoring to get there we found ourselves in water three fathoms deep.[5] And since it was nighttime, we did not dare to land, because since we had seen so many smoke spires,

1. Another two days (Oviedo 589b).

2. The Mississippi.

3. The Spanish *braza* corresponds roughly to the English fathom. The *braza* equals 5.5 feet, or 1.67 meters (Hemming 518; DRAE 201b). Evidently extending a rope about 165 feet (50 meters) down into the water, the men were unable to touch bottom.

4. One (Oviedo 589b).

5. About 16.5 feet (5 meters).

we believed that some danger might befall us without our being able to see what we ought to do, because of the great darkness. And for this reason we decided to wait until morning, and as the dawn broke each raft found itself separated from the others. I found myself in thirty fathoms of water, and continuing my course to the hour of vespers,[1] I saw two rafts,[2] and as I went toward them I saw that the first one I came upon was that of the governor, who asked me what it seemed to me we ought to do. I told him that he should catch up with the raft that went before us, and that in no way should he leave it, and that together all three of our rafts would follow along whatever path God might choose to carry us. He told me that that could not be done because the raft was very far out to sea and he wished to return to land, and that if I wanted to follow it[3] I should have my men take their oars and row, because only by the strength of arms could land be taken. And a captain whom he carried with him, called Pantoja,[4] advised him to do this, saying that if he did not reach land that day, he would not do so in six more, and in that length of time death by starvation would be inevitable. Knowing his will, I took my oar and all those on my raft who were able did the same, and we rowed almost until sunset. But since the governor carried the healthiest and most robust men among us, in no way were we able to follow or keep up with him. Having seen this, I asked him if he would allow me to attach my raft to his so that I might be able to keep up with him, and he responded that they themselves would have to expend no little effort if they alone were to reach land that night. I told him that since I saw the small possibility

1. Midday. According to Oviedo (590a), the rafts were sighted at midday.

2. The raft of Narváez and Pantoja and that of Téllez and Peñalosa.

3. The governor's raft.

4. Cabeza de Vaca refers here to Pantoja as though he had not been mentioned earlier (f3v).

we had to be able to follow him and do what he had commanded, he should tell me what it was that he ordered me to do. He answered me that it was no longer time for one man to rule another, that each one should do whatever seemed best to him in order to save his own life, [and] that he intended so to do it. And saying this he veered away with his raft.[1] And since I was unable to follow him, I headed for the other raft that was at sea, which waited for me. And upon approaching it, I discovered that it was the one that carried Captains Peñalosa and Téllez. And thus we sailed for four days together, eating as rations each day half a handful of raw maize. At the end of these four days, a storm overtook us and caused us to lose the other raft, and because of the great mercy God had for us, we did not sink in spite of the foul weather. And with it being winter and the cold very great and so many days that we suffered hunger along with the blows that we had received from the sea, the next day the people began to faint in such a manner that when the sun set all those who came in my raft were fallen on top of one another in it, so close to death that few were conscious. And among all of them at this hour there were not five men left standing. And when night came, only the helmsman and I were still able to guide the raft. And two hours into the night, the helmsman told me that I should take charge of it, because he was in such condition that he thought he would die that very night. And thus I took the tiller, and after midnight I went to see if he was dead. And he answered me that, on the contrary, he was feeling better and would steer until daybreak.

1. Cabeza de Vaca's testimony in the Joint Report moved Oviedo (590a) to contrast Narváez's self-interest with the selfless heroism of "that memorable count of Niebla, Don Enrique de Guzmán, who, in order to save others, bringing them onto his boat, filled it with so many that he and they drowned at Gibraltar." The count of Niebla was praised by Juan de Mena in his *Trescientas* (stanzas 160–85).

Certainly, at that hour I would have willingly chosen to die rather than to see so many people before me in that condition. And after the helmsman took charge of the raft, I lay down for a short time without being able to rest at all, nor was there anything farther from me at that moment than sleep. Later, near dawn, it seemed to me that I was hearing the rise and fall of the sea because, since the coast was a shoal,[1] the waves broke loudly. And with this startlement, I called the helmsman, who replied that he thought we were near land.[2] And we took a sounding and found ourselves in seven fathoms[3] of water. And it seemed to him that we should stay at sea until daybreak. And thus I took an oar and rowed on the land side as we were a league away from it, and we turned the stern toward the sea. And near land a wave took us that pitched the raft out of the water the distance of a horseshoe's throw,[4] and with the great blow that its fall occasioned, almost all the people who were nearly dead upon it regained consciousness. And since they saw themselves near land, they began to leave the raft half walking, half crawling. And as they came on land to some bluffs, we made a fire and toasted some of the maize that we carried. And we found rainwater, and with the heat of the fire the men revived and began to regain strength. The day we arrived here was the sixth of the month of November.[5]

[a]After the men had eaten, I ordered Lope de Oviedo, who was healthier and stronger than the rest, to go to some trees that were near there and, climbing one of them, to survey the land in which we found ourselves, and to try to gain some information about it. He did so and discovered that we were on an island.[6] And he saw that the land was rutted in the way that it usually is

a.] Z: *om*. V: Chapter eleven: Of what happened to Lope de Oviedo with some Indians.

1. *baxa*. Archaic for *bajío* (DRAE 156c); see (f5v).

2. The raft was approaching the Texas coast near Galveston Bay.

3. About 38.5 feet (11.7 meters).

4. *juego de herradura*.

5. The temporal references in the narration to the raft journey suggest that the date was somewhere between 11 and 18 November. Factoring in ten days to adjust for the nearly ten days that the Julian calendar had wandered from the solar year, the season probably more closely resembled that of modern early December.

6. Directly south of Galveston Island at Galveston Bay, Texas. Cabeza de Vaca will call the island Malhado (f24r).

where cattle roam, and it seemed to him for this reason that it must be land inhabited by Christians, and thus he reported it to us. I ordered him to look again more carefully and see if in this land there were any roads that could be followed, and to do this without going too far away because of the danger that there might be. He left, and coming upon a trail, he went ahead along it for the distance of half a league. And he found some Indian huts that were deserted, because the Indians[1] had gone into the countryside. And he took one of their pots and a small dog and a few mullet, and thus he returned to us. And since it seemed to us that he delayed in returning, I sent two other Christians to look for him and find out what had happened to him. And they came upon him near there, and they saw that three Indians with bows and arrows were following him, calling to him, and he in turn was calling to them with gestures. And thus he arrived to where we were, and the Indians stayed back a little, seated on the same bank. And half an hour later, another one hundred[2] Indian archers arrived, and now, whether or not they were of great stature, our fear made them seem like giants. And they stopped near us, where the first three were. It was out of the question for us to think that anyone could defend himself, since it was difficult to find even six who could raise themselves from the ground. The inspector and I went to the Indians and called them. And they came up to us, and as best we could, we tried to assure them and reassure ourselves. And we gave them beads and bells and each one of them gave me an arrow, which is a sign of friendship. And by gestures they told us that they would return in the morning and bring us food to eat because at that time they had none.

1. Members of one of the two groups—those of Capoques or of Han—that inhabited the island (f26v, f44r).

2. Two hundred (Oviedo 590b).

a.] Z: *om.* V: Chapter twelve:
How the Indians brought us
food.

c. had said] V: had told us

[a]The next day at sunrise, which was the hour the Indians had said,[c] they came to us as they had promised, and they brought us much fish and some roots that they eat, which are like nuts, some larger, some smaller; the majority of them they dig out from under water with great difficulty. In the afternoon they returned and brought us more fish and some of the same roots. And they had their women and children come to see us, and thus they went home rich in the bells and beads that we gave them. And on subsequent days they returned to visit us, bringing the same things as on previous occasions. Since we found ourselves provided with fish and roots and water and the other things we requested, we resolved to embark again and continue on our journey. And we dug the raft out of the sand in which it was stuck. And it was necessary for us to undress and endure great labor in order to launch it, because we were in such a condition that other much less strenuous tasks would have sufficed to place us in difficulty. And thus embarked, at a distance of two crossbow shots out to sea, we were hit by such a huge wave that we were all soaked, and since we went naked and the cold was very great, we dropped the oars from our hands. And with a successive wave the sea overturned our raft. The inspector and two others clung to it in order to save themselves, but the result was quite the opposite, for the raft dragged them under and drowned them.[1] Since the shoreline is very rugged, the sea, with a single thrust, threw all the others, who were in the waves and half drowned, onto the coast of the same island[2] without the loss of any more than the three whom the raft had taken under. Those of us who escaped [were]

1. Cabeza de Vaca gives the first account of a raft to sink; it was his own. The inspector, Alonso (Diego) de Solís, with whom he had shared the command on the raft from the Bay of Horses (f16r), and two other men were drowned.

2. Malhado.

naked as the day we were born and [we had] lost everything we carried with us. And although all of it was of little value, at that time it was worth a great deal. And since it was November and the cold very great, we, so thin that with little difficulty our bones could be counted, appeared like the figure of death itself. For myself I can say that since the month of May I had not eaten any other thing but toasted maize, and sometimes I found myself having to eat it raw, because although the horses were killed during the time the rafts were being constructed, I could never eat of them,[1] and there were not more than ten occasions on which I ate fish. I say this by way of explanation so that each one might understand the conditions in which we found ourselves. And beyond all this, a north wind came up, bringing us closer to death than to life. God granted that while looking for firebrands from the fire that we had built there, we discovered a flame with which we made great bonfires. And thus we were beseeching our Lord for mercy and the pardon of our sins, shedding many tears, each one having pity not only for himself but for all the others whom they saw in the same state. And at the hour of sunset, the Indians, believing that we had not gone away, came back to look for us and bring us food. But when they saw us in this manner and dressed so differently from the first time, and in such a strange state, they were so frightened that they withdrew. I ran after them and called them, and they came back very frightened. I made them understand through gestures how a raft had sunk on us and three members of our company had drowned. And there in their presence they themselves saw two dead men, and those of us who remained were traveling that same road. The Indians, on seeing the disaster that had

1. Oviedo (588a) states that some of the men had helped construct the rafts for the sole purpose of being allowed to eat some of the horse meat.

befallen us and the disaster that was upon us with so much misfortune and misery, sat down among us. And with the great grief and pity they felt on seeing us in such a state, they all began to weep loudly and so sincerely that they could be heard a great distance away.[1] And this lasted more than half an hour, and truly, to see that these men, so lacking in reason and so crude in the manner of brutes, grieved so much for us, increased in me and in others of our company even more the magnitude of our suffering and the estimation of our misfortune. When this weeping was somewhat[c] calmed, I asked the Christians and said that, if it seemed acceptable to them, I would ask those Indians to take us to their houses. And some of them who had been in New Spain replied that we should not even speak of it, because if they took us to their houses, they would sacrifice us to their idols.[2] But realizing that there was no other solution, and that by any other course death was closer and more certain, I did not heed their words, but rather beseeched the Indians to take us to their houses. And they showed that they took great pleasure in this, and that we should wait a little while, that they would do what we wanted. And later, thirty of them gathered firewood and went to their houses, which were far away from there. And we remained with the others until close to nightfall, when they took us, and by their carrying us by clutching us tightly and making great haste, we went to their houses. And because of the great cold, and fearing that on the road some one of us might fall unconscious or die, they made provision for four or five very great bonfires placed at intervals, and at each one they warmed us; and when they saw that we had regained some strength and warmth, they carried us to the next one, so rapidly that they almost did not let our feet touch the ground. And in this

c. somewhat] V: *om.*

1. Cabeza de Vaca (f24v, f26v) later describes ritual weeping among these coastal peoples of the northwestern Gulf of Mexico.

2. A number of the men on this expedition were veterans of the conquest of Mexico (1519–21), including many who had accompanied Narváez to Mexico in 1520 to oppose Cortés. Juan Suárez was one of the first Franciscan missionaries to New Spain, arriving there in 1524 (f3r).

Rumor and knowledge of human sacrifice among the Mexica (Aztecs) circulated throughout the Hispanic world.

a. neither] V: neither pleasure,

d.] Z: *om.* V: Chapter thirteen: How we learned of other Christians.

manner we went to their houses, where we found that they had prepared a house for us and many fires in it. And an hour after we arrived, they began to dance and make a great celebration that lasted all night long, although for us there was neither[a] rejoicing nor sleep, as we were awaiting the moment when they would sacrifice us. And in the morning they again gave us fish and roots and treated us so well that we were somewhat reassured, and we lost some of our fear of being sacrificed.

[d]This same day I saw on one of those Indians an item of barter and I knew that it was not from the ones that we had given them. And asking where those items had been acquired, they responded to me by signs that other men like us who were farther back[1] had given it to him. Seeing this, I sent two Christians and two Indians to show them those people, and very near there they came upon them, and they were also coming to look for us, because the Indians who lived there had told them about us, and these men were the captains Andrés Dorantes and Alonso del Castillo with all the men of their raft. Upon encountering us, they received a great fright to see us in the condition we were in. And it gave them great sorrow not to have anything to give us, because they brought no clothing other than what they were wearing. And they remained there with us and told us how on the fifth day of that same month their raft had capsized a league and a half from there, and they had escaped without losing anything.[2] And all together we agreed to repair their raft, to go forward in it those of us who had the strength and will to

1. *atrás.* Farther back on the island of Malhado, that is, in the direction of the Florida Peninsula. From this point in the narration, Cabeza de Vaca uses the term *atrás* (back) in the same sense as "la vía de la Florida" (the way of *Florida*). The opposite, *adelante* (forward), is equivalent to "la vía de Palmas" (the way of Palms) or "la vía de Pánuco" (the way of Pánuco) and refers to movement toward the mouths of the Río de las Palmas and the Río Pánuco.

2. On 5 November 1528 (Oviedo 591b), Dorantes and Castillo's raft had landed on Malhado, but nearer the Florida end of the island than that of Cabeza de Vaca. Here Cabeza de Vaca accounts for the second of the five rafts.

do so, the others to remain there until they recovered to the point where they could go along the coast as they were able, and wait there until God should take them with us to the land of Christians. And as we contemplated it, so we put it into effect. And before we had launched the raft, Tavera, a man of gentle birth from our company, died. And the raft we planned to take met its end, and it could not remain afloat and later was sunk. And as we remained in the circumstances that I have described, with most of the men naked and the weather too severe to walk and swim across rivers and bays, and without any provisions or the means to carry them, we decided to do what necessity dictated, which was to spend the winter there. And we also agreed that four of the most hearty men should go to Pánuco, believing that we were near there, and that if God our Lord should see fit to carry them there, they should give notice of how we remained on that island and of our great need and hardships. These men were very great swimmers:[1] and one was named Álvaro Fernández, a Portuguese carpenter and sailor;[2] the second was called Méndez; and the third, Figueroa, who was a native of Toledo; the fourth, Estudillo,[d] a native of Zafra. They took with them an Indian from the island of Avia.[f3]

g[These] four Christians having departed, a few days later the weather turned so cold and there were such great storms that the Indians could not pull up the roots. And from the waterways[i4] where they fished there was no yield whatsoever. And as the houses were so unprotected, the people began to die. And five men who were in Xamho[j] on the coast came to such

d. Estudillo] V: Astudillo

f. of Avia] V: *om.*

g.] Z: *om.* V: Chapter fourteen: How four Christians departed.

i. waterways] V: weirs

j. in Xamho] V: encamped

1. Most of the expeditionaries' inability to swim was a great hindrance to them and is mentioned by Cabeza de Vaca on other occasions (f28r, f29v). Oviedo (598b) referred to two of the most successful travelers among the survivors—Figueroa (mentioned here) and another, the Asturian cleric (see f27r)—as "chripstianos nadadores" (Christians who knew how to swim).

2. See (f15v).

3. *de Avia.* This reference, omitted from the Valladolid (1555) edition, is unidentified. The four Christians and the Indian left Malhado in late 1528.

4. "Waterways" (*canales*) in the Zamora (1542) edition, "weirs" (*cañales*) in the Valladolid (1555). The latter are fences or enclosures set in waterways for taking fish; it is unclear whether these Indians constructed such traps.

dire need that they ate one another until only one remained, who because
he was alone, had no one to eat him. The names of these men were: Sierra,
Diego López, Corral, Palacios, Gonzalo Ruiz. The Indians became very upset
because of this and it produced such a great scandal among them that without
a doubt, if at the start they had seen it, they would have killed them, and all of
us would have been in grave danger. Finally, in a very short time, of us eighty
men who arrived there from both ends [of the island], only fifteen remained
alive.[1] And after these men had died, a stomach ailment befell the Indians
of the land, from which half of them died. And they thought that we were
the ones who had killed them. And taking this to be very true, they planned
among themselves to kill those of us who remained. When they came to put
it into effect, an Indian in whose possession I had been placed told them that
they should not believe that we were the ones who killed them, because if we
had such power, we would not have allowed so many of our own to die, as
they saw, without our being able to prevent it, and that since no more than
a few of us now remained, and since none of us did any harm or ill, the best
thing to do would be to leave us alone. And our Lord God granted that the
others followed this advice and opinion, and thus they were diverted from
their intention. To this island we gave the name Malhado.[2] The people[3] we
found there are large and well proportioned. They have no weapons other
than bows and arrows, which they employ with great skill. The men have
one pierced nipple and some have both pierced. And through the hole they
make, they wear a reed up to two and a half spans[4] long

1. Cabeza de Vaca (f27r) later
gives the names of fifteen men
besides himself who survived
the winter of 1528–29 in the
region of Malhado. Oviedo
(593b) mentions one additional
survivor whose name is not
given.

2. Oviedo (615a) points out
that the three hidalgos did
not name the island in the
Joint Report, and he objects to
Cabeza de Vaca's coining the
name "Isle of Ill Fate" (Mal
Hado).

3. The Indians of Capoques
and of Han (f26v, f44r).

4. See (f13r).

a. waterways] V: weirs

and as thick as two fingers.[1] They also have their lower lip pierced and a piece of reed as thin as half a finger placed in it. The women are given to hard work. They inhabit this island from October to the end of February. They sustain themselves on the roots that I have mentioned, which they dig out from under water in November and December. They have waterways[a2] and they do not have fish apart from this period; from then on they eat the roots. At the end of February they go to other places to look for food because at that time the roots begin to sprout and become inedible. These people love their children more and treat them better than any other people in the world. And when it happens that one of their children dies, the parents and the relatives and all the rest of the people weep. And the weeping lasts a whole year, that is, each day in the morning before sunrise, first the parents begin to weep, and after this the entire community also weeps. And they do this at noon, and at daybreak. And after a year of mourning has passed, they perform the honors of the dead and wash and cleanse themselves of the ashes they wear. They mourn all the dead in this manner, except for the elderly, to whom they pay no attention, because they say they have lived past their time, and from them no gain is to be had, rather, they occupy land and deprive the children of their share of the food. Their custom is to bury their dead, except those among them who are physicians,[3] whose remains they burn. And while the fire burns, they all dance and make a great celebration. And afterward they pulverize the bones. And a year later, upon paying homage to them, they all lacerate themselves, and to the

1. *dedo*. A measurement of approximately 18 millimeters (somewhat less than an inch) (DRAE 425c).

2. See (f23v).

3. *físico*. For the definition of *físico*, see (f25v).

relatives they give the powdered bones so that they may drink them in water. Each of them has one wife.[1] Among them, the physicians are the most unconstrained; they can have two or three wives, among whom there is great friendship and harmony. When one gives his daughter in marriage, from the day that the one who takes her as his wife marries her, everything that he kills hunting or fishing is taken by his wife to the house of her father without daring to take or eat anything of it. And from the house of the father-in-law, food is brought to the husband, and in all this time [neither] the father-in-law nor the mother-in-law enters his house, nor is he to enter the house of any of his in-laws. And if it should happen that they meet anywhere, they veer a crossbow's shot from their course, and as they go distancing themselves from one another, they carry their heads lowered and their eyes to the ground, because they consider it a bad thing to see or speak with one another. The women are at liberty to communicate and converse with their parents-in-law and relatives. And this custom is common from the island [of Malhado] to more than fifty leagues inland. They have another custom, which is that when a child or a sibling dies, in the household in which the death occurs they cease to seek food for three months, but rather they allow themselves to starve. And their relatives and neighbors supply them with the food they are to eat. And because in the time we were there so many of them died, in most of the houses there was very great hunger in the effort to also keep their custom and ceremony. And those who sought food, in spite of their great labors, could find but very little, because the weather was so severe. And for this reason, the Indians who held me left the island, and in some

1. *mujer conocida*. A woman recognized by the group as belonging to a particular man.

canoes crossed to the mainland to certain bays that had many oysters. And for three months of the year they eat nothing else and drink very bad water.[1] There is a great scarcity of firewood, and there are mosquitoes in great abundance. Their houses are built of woven reeds on top of beds of oyster shells. And they sleep on them on animal skins, if they happen to have them.[2] And thus we were there until the end of April when we went to the seacoast where we ate blackberries[3] the entire month, during which time they do not[a] cease to perform their *areitos*[4] and celebrations.

[b][5]On that island about which I have spoken, they tried to make us physicians[6] without examining us or asking us for our titles, because they cure illnesses by blowing on the sick person, and with that breath of air and their hands they expel the disease from him. And they demanded that we do the same and make ourselves useful. We laughed about this, saying that it was a mockery and that we did not know how to cure. And because of this, they took away our food until we did as they told us. And seeing our resistance, an Indian told me that I didn't know what I was saying when I said that what he knew how to do would do no good, because the stones and other things that the fields produce have powers, and that he, by placing a hot stone on the abdomen, restored health and removed pain, and that it was certain that we, because we were men, had greater virtue and capacity. In short, we found ourselves in such need that we had to do it, without fearing that anyone would bring us to grief for it. The manner in which they perform cures is as follows: on becoming sick, they call a physician and

a. do not] Z: *om.*

b.] Z: *om.* V: Chapter fifteen: Of what happened to us in the *villa* of Malhado.

1. Oviedo (592a) describes this as "salobre," or salt water. Both accounts speak of the shortage of water, the collection of rainwater, and the natives' movement in search of it in these coastal saltwater regions.

2. Cabeza de Vaca makes many references to the use of deerskins by the coastal Indians (f26v–f40v) and describes the manner of hunting deer among groups farther down the coast from Galveston Bay (f33v). Oviedo (601a) also describes the hunting of deer among these same groups, who drove them into the water, where they would drown.

3. *moras de zarzas.* Literally, blackberries, black dewberries, according to Coopwood (116).

4. Ritual song and dance, in the Taino language of the Caribbean.

5. This title (probably added by a typesetter or editor, given its erroneous content) indicates that the Spanish established a municipality (*villa*) on Malhado, which was not the case.

6. *físico.* "He who professes the science of the nature of things and knows their qualities and properties" (Covarrubias 597a). According to the *Siete partidas* (Castile 1:f24r–v [pt. 2, tit. 9, law 10]), it is "knowledge of the nature of things and their interactions; knowing such things, one can do much good and remove evil, particularly preserving the life and health of men and preventing them from falling ill." For Cabeza de Vaca's description of native shamans of the island, see (f24v–f25r). Oviedo (603b) says the men did not begin curing until they reached groups beyond the Avavares more than six years later.

after being cured they not only give him everything they possess, but they also seek things to give him from among their relatives. What the physician does is to make some incisions where the sick person has pain, and then sucks all around them. They perform cauterizations with fire, which is a thing among them considered to be very effective, and I have tried it and it turned out well for me. And after this, they blow upon the area that hurts, and with this they believe that they have removed the malady. The manner in which we performed cures was by making the sign of the cross over them and blowing on them, and praying a Pater Noster and an Ave Maria, and as best we could, beseeching our Lord God that he grant them health and move them to treat us well. Our Lord God in his mercy willed that all those on whose behalf we made supplication, after we had made the sign of the cross over them, said to the others that they were restored and healthy, and on account of this they treated us well, and refrained from eating in order to give their food to us, and they gave us skins and other things. The hunger that we suffered there was so extreme that many times I went three days without eating anything, and they also suffered the same, and it seemed impossible to me to remain alive, although many times afterward, I found myself in even greater hunger and necessity, as I will recount later.

The Indians who held Alonso del Castillo and Andrés Dorantes and the others who had remained alive, since they spoke another language and were of a different lineage, crossed to a different part of the mainland to eat oysters, and they remained there until the first day of the month of April,[1] and afterward they returned to the island, which is probably about two leagues from there at the point where the water is the widest, and the island is a half league wide and five long. All the people of this land go about naked. Only the women cover part of their bodies with a type of fiber that grows on trees. The young women cover themselves with deerskins. They are people who freely share what they have with one another. There is no lord among them. All who are of a single lineage band together. On the island live people of two different languages: some are called of Capoques, and the others, of Han. They have as a custom that, when they know one another and meet from time to time, before they speak they weep for half an hour, and when this is done, the one who receives the visit rises first and gives to the other everything he possesses, and the other receives it. And a little while later he goes away with it, and it even happens sometimes that after receiving the goods, they part without speaking a single word. They have other strange customs, but I have told the most important and most notable ones so that I may go on and tell what else happened to us.

^cAfter Dorantes and Castillo returned to the island, they gathered together all the Christians who were somewhat dispersed, and found them to be fourteen in number.[2] As I have said, I was on the other side, on the mainland, where my Indians had taken me and where a great sickness had befallen me, such that if any other thing were to give me hope of survival, that illness alone sufficed to deprive me of it altogether. And when the

c.] Z: *om.* V: Chapter sixteen: How the Christians departed from the island of Malhado.

1. 1529.

2. Including themselves, since they left two men on Malhado when they and ten other men departed from the island. See (f24r, f27r).

Christians found this out, they gave to an Indian the cloak of sable skins that we had taken from the cacique,[1] as we mentioned above, so that he would cross them over to where I was to see me. And thus twelve of them came, because two had become so weakened that they did not dare to bring them with them. The names of those who came over at that time are: Alonso del Castillo, Andrés Dorantes, and Diego Dorantes, Valdivieso,[2] Estrada, Tostado, Chaves, Gutiérrez, the Asturian cleric,[3] Diego de Huelva, the black man[4] Estevanico, [and] Benítez. And having arrived on the mainland, they found another one of our men named Francisco de León. And all thirteen went along the coast.[5] And after they had crossed, the Indians who held me informed me of it, and of how Jerónimo de Alaniz[6] and Lope de Oviedo[7] had remained on the island. My sickness prevented me from following them, nor did I see them. I had to remain with these same Indians from the island for more than a year,[8] and because of the great labors they forced me to perform and the bad treatment they gave me, I resolved to flee from them and go to those who live in the forests and on the mainland, who are called those of Charruco, because I was unable to endure the life that I had with these others; because among many other tasks, I had to dig the roots to eat out from under the water and among the rushes where they grew in the ground. And because of this, my fingers were so worn that when a reed touched them it caused them to bleed, and the reeds cut me in many places because many of them were broken, and I had to enter into the thick of them with the clothes I have said I was wearing.[9] And because of this, I set to the

1. See (f17v). Oviedo (593a) says that the Christians paid with "certain things" (*ciertas cosas*).

2. Pedro de Valdivieso. Both Diego Dorantes and Valdivieso were cousins of Andrés Dorantes (Oviedo 598b).

3. *clérigo*. "One who receives holy orders" (DRAE 311a), impossible to identify more specifically, possibly one of the Franciscan friars on the expedition.

4. *el negro*. Cabeza de Vaca (f67r) will identify Estevanico as an Arabic-speaking native of Azemmour. Cabeza de Vaca and Oviedo (610a) confirm that Estevanico was a Christian. In 1526 a royal decree sought to control the number of *negros*

ladinos (acculturated, Spanish-speaking black Africans) brought to the Indies (see f18r) by requiring their owners to obtain special permission to take them, as Estevanico's master, Andrés Dorantes, may have had to do.

5. The group departed from the region of Malhado in the spring of 1529.

6. The notary (f7r).

7. The same one Cabeza de Vaca had ordered to climb a tree and survey the land when his men arrived at Malhado (f20v).

8. Evidently until sometime in 1530.

9. Cabeza de Vaca was "naked as the day he was born" (f21v, f22r; see also f28r, f36v, f39v, f40r, f58v).

task of going over to the others, and with them things were somewhat better for me. And because I became a merchant, I tried to exercise the vocation as best I knew how. And because of this they gave me food to eat and treated me well, and they importuned me to go from one place to another to obtain the things they needed, because on account of the continual warfare in the land, there is little traffic or communication among them. And with my dealings and wares I entered inland as far as I desired, and I went along the coast for forty or fifty leagues. The mainstay of my trade was pieces of snail shell and the hearts of them; and conch shells with which they cut a fruit that is like frijoles, with which they perform cures and do their dances and make celebrations (and this is the thing of greatest value that there is among them); and beads of the sea[1] and other things. Thus, all this is what I carried inland. And in exchange and as barter for it, I brought forth hides and red ocher with which they smear themselves and dye their faces and hair, flints to make the points of arrows, paste, and stiff canes to make them, and some tassels made from deer hair which they dye red. And this occupation served me well, because practicing it, I had the freedom to go wherever I wanted, and I was not constrained in any way nor enslaved, and wherever I went they treated me well and gave me food out of want for my wares, and most importantly because doing that, I was able to seek out the way by which I would go forward.[2] And among them I was very well known; when they saw me and I brought them the things they needed, they were greatly pleased.

1. *cuentas de la mar.* Probably pearls, since Cabeza de Vaca (f25v) observed that the Indians of the region around Galveston Bay consumed oysters and dwelt upon oyster-shell middens.

2. *adelante.* Like those who had departed from Malhado before him, Cabeza de Vaca's intention was to travel along the coast in the direction of the Río Pánuco in search of the Spanish outpost of Santisteban del Puerto located near the river's mouth (f23r).

And those who did not know me desired and endeavored to see me because of my renown. It would take long to tell the hardships that I suffered in this, not to mention the great dangers and hunger, as well as storms and cold, many of which took me in the countryside and alone, from which I escaped thanks to the boundless mercy of God our Lord. And for this reason, I did not ply my trade in winter, on account of it being the time when even they, staying inside their huts and shelters, could neither support nor protect themselves. The time that I spent in this land, alone among them and as naked as they, was nearly six years.[1] The reason I stayed so long was to take with me a Christian who was on the island, named Lope de Oviedo. His companion, [Jerónimo] de Alaniz, who had stayed with him when Alonso del Castillo and Andrés Dorantes left with all the others, had since died.[2] And in order to take him out of there, I crossed over to the island every year and begged that we go, in the best manner that we could, in search of Christians. And every year he kept me from going, saying that we would go the following year. In the end I took him. And I carried him across the inlet and four rivers that are along the coast, because he did not know how to swim.[3] And thus we went forward with some Indians[4] until we arrived at an inlet that is a league wide and deep throughout, and because of what it seemed to us and we saw, it is the one they call Espíritu Santo.[5] And from the other side of it we saw some Indians[6] who were coming to see ours,[7] and they told us that farther ahead there were three men like us, and they told us their names.[8] And asking them about the rest of them, they replied to us that they had all died of cold and hunger, and that those Indians ahead[9] had, for their own amusement, killed Diego Dorantes and Valdivieso and Diego de

1. Cabeza de Vaca probably dwelt alone among the Indians in the region of Malhado from the winter of 1528 until the time when he fled from them in the spring of 1533, that is, for a period of under four and a half years. Oviedo (598b) said that it had been five years since the other Christians had left Cabeza de Vaca at Malhado, although, in fact, it had been only four, from the spring of 1529 to the spring of 1533.

2. Alaniz's death would have occurred sometime between the springs of 1529 and 1533.

3. Cabeza de Vaca and Lope de Oviedo departed from Malhado in the spring of 1533, traveling down the coast from Galveston Bay to Matagorda Bay. Ponton and McFarland identified the four rivers as Oyster Creek, the Brazos River, the San Bernard River, and Caney Creek, the main channel of the Colorado River in the sixteenth century.

4. Deaguanes (f28v).

5. Both Cabeza de Vaca and the thirteen-man party that went down the coast before him associated the large inlet (*ancón*) with the name Espíritu Santo (Oviedo 592b, 593b, 594b), pertaining to a river and bay between the Río de las Palmas and the Florida Cape, the identity of which has never been clearly established. Although the name has often been associated with the Mississippi River, the Narváez expeditionaries seem to have applied it to Matagorda Bay. Espíritu Santo was believed in the 1520s to lie two hundred leagues toward the Florida Peninsula from the mouth of the Río Pánuco.

6. Quevenes.

7. Deaguanes.

8. Alonso del Castillo, Andrés Dorantes, and Estevanico, who in the spring of 1533 were the only survivors of the thirteen-man party that had departed from the Galveston Bay area in the spring of 1529.

9. It is difficult to determine which group of Indians was responsible for the deaths of the Spaniards. The Guaycones were the next Indians beyond the Quevenes, but from the various references in both Cabeza de Vaca's account and in Oviedo, it seems possible that other Indians farther down the coast or even the Quevenes themselves might have killed the men.

Huelva, merely because they had passed from one house to another,[1] and that the neighboring Indians,[2] with whom Captain Dorantes now was, because of a dream they had dreamed, had killed Esquivel[3] and Méndez.[4] We asked them about the condition of the ones who were alive. They told us that they were very ill treated, because the boys and other Indians, who are among them very idle and cruel, kicked and slapped and cudgeled them, and that this was the life they had among them. We tried to inform ourselves about the land that lay ahead and the provisions that were in it. They responded that it was very poorly populated, and that in it there was nothing to eat, and that the people died of cold because they had neither skins nor any other thing with which to cover themselves. They told us also that if we wanted to see those three Christians, that within two days the Indians who held them[5] would come to eat nuts[6] a league from there on the bank of that river.[7] And in order that we might see that what they had told us about the bad treatment of the others was true, while we were with them they gave my companion slaps and blows, and I did not lack my share, and they threw mud balls at us, and each day placed arrows at our hearts, saying that they wanted to kill us as they had killed our other companions. And fearing this, Lope de Oviedo, my companion, said that he wanted to go back with some women of those Indians with whom we had crossed the inlet, and who had remained a short distance back. I entreated him repeatedly not to do it, and I pointed out many things, but I was unable to detain him by any means. And thus he returned and I remained alone with those Indians, who were called Quevenes, and the others, with whom he went, are called Deaguanes.[8] [c]And

c.] Z: *om.* V: Chapter seventeen: How the Indians came forth and brought with them Andrés Dorantes and Castillo and Estevanico.

1. The deaths of these three men, as well as the fate of the entire group of thirteen men who departed from the region of Malhado in the spring of 1529 until Cabeza de Vaca joined the three survivors in the spring of 1533, are recounted in much fuller detail in Andrés Dorantes's testimony for the Joint Report, which Oviedo (593a–95a, 598b–601b) paraphrased in his account.

2. The Mariames, coastal mainland dwellers to whom some of the Spaniards (Méndez, Esquivel, Andrés Dorantes, and possibly also Diego Dorantes) fled to escape the bad treatment they received from the island-dwelling Indians.

3. Esquivel had come on the raft of the comptroller and the commissary (f30r–f31r). This early information about Esquivel was evidently the first Cabeza de Vaca received about the fate of any of those who had gone on the rafts of the comptroller/commissary and Narváez/Pantoja.

4. One of the four Narváez expeditionaries sent from Malhado in search of Pánuco in November 1528 (f23v).

5. Dorantes was being held by the Mariames, Castillo and Estevanico by the Yguases.

6. Wild pecans, likened by Cabeza de Vaca (f29r) to the "nuts of Galicia."

7. The confluence of the San Antonio and Guadalupe Rivers.

8. Also identified as "de Aguanes" (f42v), of which "Deaguanes" seems to be a contraction, the name signifying "from Aguanes."

two days after Lope de Oviedo had gone, the Indians[1] who held Alonso del Castillo and Andrés Dorantes came to the same place they had told us about to eat of those nuts, on which they sustain themselves by grinding some small granules with them for two months of the year without eating any other thing. And even this they do not have every year, because the trees bear fruit one year but not the next. They are the size of those of Galicia, and the trees are very large and there is a great number of them. An Indian informed me that the Christians had arrived, and that if I wanted to see them I should steal away and flee to the edge of a woods that he indicated to me, because he and other relatives of his had to go to see those Indians, and they would take me with them to where the Christians were. I trusted them and decided to do it, because they had a language different from that of my Indians.[2] And put into effect, the next day they went, and found me in the place that was indicated, and thus they took me with them. When I arrived near to where they had their dwelling, Andrés Dorantes came out to see who it was, because the Indians had also told him that a Christian was coming. And when he saw me, he was greatly astonished, because it had been many days[3] that they had taken me for dead, and so the Indians had told him. We gave many thanks to God upon finding ourselves reunited, and this day was one of the days of greatest pleasure that we have had in our lives. And arriving to where Castillo was, they asked me what my intentions were. I told him that my purpose was to go to the land of Christians and that on this path and pursuit I was embarked. Andrés Dorantes responded that it had been many days since he had beseeched

1. Yguases and Mariames.

2. Quevenes.

3. Cabeza de Vaca had been separated from Dorantes and the others since the spring of 1529, that is, for a period of about four years (f28r).

Castillo and Estevanico to go forward, and that they did not dare to do it because they did not know how to swim, and that they greatly feared the rivers and inlets they had to cross, which in that land are many. And since God our Lord had been served by preserving me through so many hardships and sicknesses and finally by bringing me to their company, they decided to flee, I carrying them across the rivers and inlets that we might encounter. And they advised me that by no means was I to tell the Indians nor give them reason to suspect that I wanted to go on ahead, because then they would kill me, and that for this purpose it was necessary that I remain with them for six months,[1] which was the time in which those Indians would go to another land to eat prickly pears[2] (this is a fruit the size of an egg, and they are vermilion and black and of very good flavor; they eat them three months out of the year,[3] during which time they eat nothing else), because at the time that they harvested them, other Indians from farther on[4] would come to them, bringing bows to trade and exchange with them, and that when they returned, we would flee from our Indians and return with them.[5] With this plan I remained there, and they gave me as a slave to an Indian with whom Dorantes was staying.[e] These Indians are called Marianes, and Castillo was with others, their neighbors, called Yguases. And being there, they told me[6] that after they left the island of Malhado, on the seacoast they found the raft[7] in which the comptroller and the friars had capsized, and that going across those rivers, which are four very large ones and of many currents,[8]

e. staying] V: staying, who was blind in one eye, as was his wife and a son that he had as well as another person who was in his company, to the effect that all of them were blind in one eye.

1. From about April until September 1533; Cabeza de Vaca makes two further references to this same six-month period of waiting (f33r, f34r).

2. Tuna, the Taino word for the fruit of certain cactus species. See also (f33r, f34v–f35r).

3. One and a half to two months (Oviedo 601a) or fifty to sixty days (Oviedo 601b).

4. Avavares.

5. Andrés Dorantes, Alonso del Castillo, and Estevanico had unsuccessfully attempted to escape toward Pánuco in this manner the previous year (Oviedo 601b).

6. Here begins Dorantes and Castillo's account of what had happened to the thirteen men

since the spring of 1529, when they left Cabeza de Vaca near Malhado. Oviedo's (593a–95a, 598b–601b) version of the same events, drawn from Andrés Dorantes's testimony, gives an account of the same period but in much greater detail. Dorantes and Castillo's account ends on (f31r).

7. The fate of the third of the five rafts is revealed; it had arrived south of Malhado at the mouth of the San Bernard River in early November 1528.

8. Oyster Creek, the Brazos River, the San Bernard River, and Caney Creek (f28r).

the rafts in which they were traveling carried them out to sea where four of them drowned,[1] and that thus they went onward until they crossed the inlet,[2] and they crossed it with great difficulty. And fifteen leagues ahead they found another,[3] and when they arrived there, two of their companions had already died in the sixty leagues that they had gone, and that all those who remained were in a similar state, and that along the entire route they had not eaten anything except crayfish and kelp.[4] And having arrived at this last inlet, they said that they found in it Indians[5] who were eating blackberries, and since they saw the Christians, they went from there to another cape. And [Dorantes and Castillo told me] that being in the process of finding a way to cross the inlet, an Indian and a Christian crossed over to them, and when he had arrived, they learned that it was Figueroa, one of the four whom we had sent ahead from the island of Malhado.[6] And there he [Figueroa][7] told them [Dorantes and Castillo and the other five survivors of those who had arrived from Malhado to where he was] how he and his companions [Fernández, Estudillo, and Méndez, who had left from Malhado in November of the preceding year] had arrived to that place, where two of them and an Indian had died, all three from cold and hunger, because they had set out and traveled during the harshest weather ever seen in the world, and that the Indians[8] had taken him and Méndez, and that being with them, Méndez had fled, going along the route toward Pánuco as best he could, and that the Indians had gone after him [Méndez] and that they had killed him.[9] And [Figueroa told Dorantes, Castillo, and the other five] that being with these Indians, he learned from them that with the Mariames there was a Christian who had crossed over from the other side, and [that] he [Figueroa] had found him [the Christian] with the ones who were called Quevenes, and that this Christian was Hernando de Esquivel, a native of Badajoz, who had come in the company of the commissary. And [Figueroa told them] that he had learned from Esquivel

1. Oviedo (593b) mentions only two drownings.

2. Between Matagorda Peninsula and Matagorda Island, referred to by Cabeza de Vaca (f28r) as the inlet (*ancón*) of Espíritu Santo.

3. Between Matagorda and St. Joseph Islands.

4. *yerba pedrera*. Oviedo (593a) describes this as growing plentifully along the coast and notes its use in Spain in making glass.

5. Probably Quevenes.

6. Figueroa had left Malhado in November 1528 (f23v).

7. Here Cabeza de Vaca narrates the information that Dorantes and Castillo gave him, in 1533, about Figueroa's experiences as he had related them to Dorantes, Castillo, and their men in the spring of 1529. Figueroa's account is concluded on (f31r).

8. Quevenes.

9. Although the immediate context suggests that these Indians were Quevenes or other island groups farther down the coast, Cabeza de Vaca (f28v) earlier indicated that Méndez had been killed by the Mariames because of a dream.

about the end to which the governor and the comptroller and the others had come.[1] And he [Esquivel] told him [Figueroa] that the comptroller and the friars had capsized in their raft between the rivers,[2] and coming down along the coast, the raft of the governor landed on the shore with his men, and he [the governor] went with his raft until they arrived at that large inlet,[3] and that there he again boarded the men[4] and crossed them from the other side, and went back for the comptroller and the friars and all the others. And he [Esquivel] told how being disembarked, the governor had revoked the authority of the comptroller as his lieutenant, and he gave the command to a captain whom he had with him, named Pantoja,[5] and that the governor remained on his raft and refused that night to come on land. And a helmsman and a page[6] who was ill remained with him, and on the raft they had neither water nor anything to eat, and at midnight the north wind blew so strongly that it took the raft out to sea without anyone seeing it, because it had no grapnel[7] except for a rock, and that nothing more was ever heard of it.[8] And [Esquivel told Figueroa] that having seen this, the people who remained on land went down the coast, and that because they found such a great barrier of water,[9] with great difficulty they made small rafts in which they crossed to the other side, and that going ahead, they arrived to a point of a woods at the edge of the water, and that they found Indians[10] who, as they saw them coming, put their houses in their canoes and crossed from the other side to the coast. And the Christians, seeing the weather as it was, because it was the month of November,[11] stopped at this wood, because they found water and firewood and some crayfish and shellfish, where, from cold and from

1. Cabeza de Vaca here tells what he had learned from Dorantes and Castillo in 1533; Dorantes and Castillo had met Figueroa in 1529 and learned from him, on the basis of Esquivel's account to Figueroa earlier that same year, what had happened to Narváez's raft and that of the comptroller and the commissary in the autumn and winter of 1528.

2. Between the Brazos and the San Bernard Rivers (f29v).

3. Espíritu Santo, between Matagorda Peninsula and Matagorda Island (f30r).

4. Oviedo (594a) explicitly states that Narváez had his company disembark and walk along the shore. This is not completely evident here.

5. Pantoja has been mentioned twice before (f3v, f19v). Oviedo does not mention this detail.

6. Oviedo (594b) identifies these two as a pilot named Antón Pérez and his page, Campo.

7. *resón*. A small anchor with four or five flukes or claws.

8. The fourth raft of the five, commanded by the governor and Captain Pantoja; it had been swept out to sea sometime in November 1528.

9. Between Matagorda and St. Joseph Islands.

10. Quevenes or others farther ahead.

11. 1528.

hunger, they began little by little to die. Beyond this, Pantoja, who had remained as lieutenant,[1] treated them very badly. And not being able to endure it, Sotomayor[2] (the brother of Vasco Porcallo, the one from the island of Cuba), who had come on the expedition as camp master, set against him and gave Pantoja such a blow that it killed him, and thus they went on dying. And the flesh of those who died was jerked[3] by the others. And the last one to die was Sotomayor, and Esquivel made jerky of him, and eating of him [of Sotomayor], he [Esquivel] maintained himself until the first of March,[4] when an Indian of those who had fled from there came to see if they were dead, and he took Esquivel with him. And while he [Esquivel] was in the custody of this Indian, Figueroa spoke to him. And he [Figueroa] learned from him [from Esquivel] all that we have told. And he [Figueroa] urged him [Esquivel] to come with him to go together along the route to Pánuco, which Esquivel refused to do, saying that he had learned from the friars that Pánuco lay behind, and thus he remained there. And Figueroa went to the coast where he usually stayed.[5]

[d]Figueroa gave this entire account [to Dorantes, Castillo, and the other five] on the basis of the report that he had received from Esquivel, and thus it came from hand to hand to me,[6] by which can be seen and known the end that that entire expedition met, and the specific events that befell each one of the rest of them.[7] And he [Figueroa] said in addition, that if the Christians[8] wandered there for a time, that it was possible that they would see Esquivel, because he knew that he [Esquivel] had fled from that Indian with whom he was staying, to others, who were called the Mareames, who lived nearby there. And as I have just said,[9] he [Figueroa] and the Asturian attempted to go to other Indians who were farther ahead. But

---

1. Narváez's lieutenant governor. See (f30v).

2. See (f3v). As camp master (*maestre de campo*), Sotomayor would have been second-in-command of the military troops on the expedition, responsible for tactics and supply (Hemming 515).

3. *tassajar.* To jerk or preserve meat in long, sun-dried strips.

4. 1529.

5. Between November 1528 and March 1529 the Franciscan friars who had come on the expedition apparently became convinced that they had passed

their destination of Pánuco and landed to the south of it. Thus, Esquivel and Figueroa had opposing views regarding the direction of travel along the coast necessary to reach Santisteban del Puerto on the Río Pánuco.

6. That is, from Esquivel, to Figueroa, to Dorantes and Castillo, to Cabeza de Vaca.

7. Cabeza de Vaca here resumes Figueroa's account to Dorantes and Castillo after this interrupting sentence commenting on the various accounts given thus far and the manner in which he received

them (f21v, f23v, f29v, f30v). The fate of the fifth raft, commanded by Téllez and Peñalosa, has not yet been revealed.

8. The survivors of Dorantes and Castillo's thirteen-man party that left Malhado in 1529 who encountered Figueroa along the coast.

9. At this point, Cabeza de Vaca ceases to narrate in the third person his paraphrase of the various accounts Dorantes and Castillo had related to him and begins to relate the experiences of these men from the spring of 1529 until he joined them

in the spring of 1533 in the first person as though he himself had witnessed them. The account Dorantes and Castillo gave Cabeza de Vaca in 1533 is in fact the source for all this information about events preceding Cabeza de Vaca's reunion with Dorantes, Castillo, and Estevanico in 1533. Oviedo (594b–95a, 598a–601b) replaces the fragmentary details about this period that Cabeza de Vaca did not witness with the account of considerably greater detail and clarity that he wrote from Andrés Dorantes's Joint Report testimony.

since the Indians[1] who held them found out about it, they confronted them and gave them many blows and stripped the Asturian and passed an arrow through his arm. And in the end they escaped, fleeing.[2] And the other[d] Christians remained with those Indians, who intimidated them in order to more easily make them their slaves,[3] although being in their service they were treated worse than slaves or men of any fate had ever been, because of the six of them, not content to slap them and strike them and pull out their beards for their amusement, for the mere reason of going from one house to another they killed three, who are those I mentioned above: Diego Dorantes, and Valdivieso, and Diego de Huelva.[4] And the other three who remained expected to meet the same end. And to not suffer this life, Andrés Dorantes fled and went over to the Mareames, who were those to whom Esquivel had gone, and they told him how they had held Esquivel there, and how, upon being there, he had tried to flee because a woman had dreamed that he was to kill a son of hers, and the Indians went after him and killed him.[5] And they showed Andrés Dorantes his sword and his beads and book[6] and other things that he had. These people do this because of a custom they have, and it is, that they kill their own children because of dreams, and when female children are born, they allow dogs to eat them, and cast them away from there. The reason they do this, according to what they say, is that all the people of the land are their enemies, and with them they have continual war, and that if by chance they should marry off their daughters, their enemies would multiply so much that they would be captured and enslaved by them, and for this reason they preferred rather

1. Quevenes or other Indians farther down the coast.

2. Oviedo (599a) recounts how Pedro de Valdivieso had seen the clothes, breviary, and journal of the Asturian in a native village through which the Asturian and Figueroa had passed, probably on the northern end of Padre Island, sometime in late 1529. See (f39v).

3. Oviedo (599a) comments that the men were taken as slaves and treated more cruelly than even a Moorish slave master would do, because apart from going naked and barefoot along that coast (which "burned like fire in the summer"), they were forced to bring firewood and water and everything else that the Indians needed and to pull the canoes about in the heat.

4. The deaths of these three were mentioned earlier (f28r–v).

5. This incident was recounted earlier (f28v).

6. Evidently a rosary and a breviary or Bible.

c. long] V: long. They kill their
own children and buy those of
other groups. Their marriages
last only as long as they are
content, and they dissolve their
marriages over the slightest
things.

e. like them] V: *om.*

to kill them, than that there be born of them those who would be their
enemies. We asked them why they did not marry them themselves and also
among one another. They said it was an ugly thing to marry them to their
relatives, and that it was much better to kill them than to give them either to
a relative or to an enemy. And these Indians and others, their neighbors who
are called the Yaguazes,[b] alone practice this custom, without any others of
the land keeping it. And when these Indians are to marry, they buy women
from their enemies, and the price that each one pays for his is a bow, the best
that can be found, with two arrows, and if by chance he has no bow, then a
net up to one fathom wide and one long.[c] (Dorantes was with these Indians,
and after a few days he fled. Castillo and Estevanico came to the mainland
to the Yeguazes.)[1] All these people are archers and well built, although not
as large as those we had left behind, and like them,[e] they have one nipple
and their lower lip pierced. Their sustenance is chiefly roots of two or three
kinds, and they hunt for them throughout the land; they are very bad and
the men who eat them bloat. They take two days to roast, and many of them
are very bitter, and with all this they dig them out with great difficulty. The
hunger that those people have is so great that they are forced to eat them, and
they roam up to two or three leagues looking for them. Sometimes they kill
some deer, and sometimes they take some fish, but this is so little and their
hunger so great that they eat spiders and ant eggs and worms and lizards
and salamanders and snakes and vipers that

1. The Indians, referred to here
as holding Dorantes before he
fled, were probably Guaycones,
insofar as the interpolation is
not related to the surrounding
text, most of which describes
the customs of the Mariames.
These sentences, interpolated
into the account of native
customs, summarize a much
more detailed account in
Oviedo (599b–601b) of Andrés
Dorantes, Castillo, Estevanico,
and Diego Dorantes's passage
over from the islands where
they were originally enslaved
to the mainland and their life
among the natives between
1529 and 1533. Cabeza de
Vaca's narrative of Dorantes
and Castillo's account to
him of their experiences
subtly ends here, subsumed
by generalized ethnographic
description and followed by
the commencement of Cabeza
de Vaca's narration of the four
men's common experience
from the spring of 1533 onward,
beginning with the six months
they waited to go to the prickly
pear grounds.

a. when they strike] V: whom
they bite

kill men when they strike,[a] and they eat earth and wood and everything that they can find and deer excrement and other things that I refrain from mentioning; and I believe assuredly that if in that land there were stones they would eat them. They keep the bones of the fish they eat and of the snakes and other things in order to grind up everything afterward and eat the powder it produces. Among these people, the men do not burden themselves nor carry anything of weight, rather, the women and the old people, who are the ones they value the least, carry it. They don't love their children as much as the ones about whom we spoke earlier. There are some among them who practice sodomy.[1] The women are very hardworking and endure a great deal, because of the twenty-four hours there are between day and night, they have only six of rest, and the rest of the night they spend in firing their ovens in order to dry those roots they eat. And from daybreak, they begin to dig and bring firewood and water to their homes, and put in order the other things of which they have need. Most of these people are great thieves, because although among one another they share a great deal, in turning one's back, one's own son or father will take whatever he can. They lie a great deal. And they are great drunkards, and for this they drink a particular thing.[2] They are so skilled in running that without resting or tiring they run from morning until night following a deer. And in this way they kill many of them, because they follow them until they tire them, and sometimes they take them alive. Their houses are of woven reeds placed upon four bows. They dismantle

e. dismantle and carry them]
V: carry them on their backs

and carry them[e] and move every two or three days in order to look for

1. *pecado contra natura.*
Sodomy and bestiality,
punishable by death (Castile
3:f72v–f73r [pt. 7, tit. 21, laws
1–2]; Lea 4:361–62).

2. See (f44v).

food. They sow nothing that they can use. They are a very happy people; in spite of the great hunger they have, they do not on that account fail to dance or to make their celebrations and *areitos*. The best season that these people have is when they eat the prickly pears, because then they are not hungry, and they spend all their time dancing and eating of them, night and day. The entire time that they last, they press them and open them and place them to dry. And after being dried, they put them in certain baskets like figs, and save them to eat along the way when they return, and they grind the skins and make a powder of them. Many times when we were with these people, we went three or four days without eating, because nothing was available. To cheer us up, they told us that we should not be sad, because soon there would be prickly pears, and we would eat many and drink of their juice, and our bellies would be very big, and we would be very content and happy and without any hunger whatsoever. And from the time that they told us this until the prickly pears were ready to eat, was five or six months. And in the end we had to wait those six months,[1] and when it was time, we went to eat the prickly pears. We found throughout the land a very great quantity of mosquitoes of three types that are very bad and vexatious, and all the rest of the summer they exhausted us. And in order to defend ourselves from them, we made around the edge of the group great bonfires of rotted and wet wood that would not burn but rather make smoke. And this defense gave us yet another hardship, because all night long we did nothing

1. Cabeza de Vaca's second mention of this waiting period, from spring to late summer 1533. On the location of the prickly pear grounds, see (f34r).

but weep from the smoke that got in our eyes, and beyond this the many fires caused us to be very hot, and we would go to sleep on the shore. And if on occasion we were able to sleep, they would remind us with blows to return to light the fires. Those from inland areas[1] use for this purpose another remedy even more intolerable than this one that I have just mentioned; and it is to walk, with torches in hand, burning the fields and woods they encounter to drive the mosquitoes away, and also to drive out from underground lizards and other similar things in order to eat them. And they also often kill deer, surrounding them with many bonfires. And they also use this to take pastureland away from the animals, since necessity forces them to go to seek it where they want, because they never set down their houses except where there is water and firewood, and sometimes they all carry these supplies and go to hunt the deer that are ordinarily found where there is no water or wood. And the day they arrive, they kill deer and whatever else they can, and they use all the water and wood in cooking what they eat and in the fires they make to protect themselves from the mosquitoes. And they wait until the next day to get something to take on their journey. And when they leave, they go in such condition from the mosquitoes that it seems that they have the sickness of Saint Lazarus.[2] And in this way they satisfy their hunger two or three times a year at as great a cost as I have said. And for having lived through it, I can affirm that no hardship endured in the world equals this one. Throughout the land there are many deer and other birds and animals of the types about which I have previously told.

1. Here Cabeza de Vaca refers not to native groups he has already encountered but rather to those living somewhat inland but still near the coastline of the Gulf of Mexico whom he would meet later.

2. Leprosy.

a. long] V: long, merino, like
an Hibernian cape.

Cows sometimes range as far as here, and three times I have seen and eaten of
them. And it seems to me that they are about the size of those of Spain.[1] They
have small horns like Moorish cows, and their fur is very long.[a] Some are
brown and others black, and in my opinion they have better meat and more
of it than those from here.[2] From [the skins] of the young ones the Indians
make robes to cover themselves, and from [the hides of] the mature animals
they make shoes and shields. These cows come from the north forward

b. over] V: over all

through the land to the coast of *Florida* and they extend over[b] the land for
more than four hundred leagues. And along this entire route throughout
the valleys through which they come, the people who inhabit them come
down and sustain themselves on them, and they supply the land with a great
quantity of hides.[3]

c.] Z: *om.* V: Chapter nineteen:
Of how the Indians separated
us.

[c]When the six months[4] that I was with the Christians were over, waiting
to put into effect the plan that we had made, the Indians went to the prickly
pears, which is from there[5] to where they were to gather them, some thirty
leagues.[6] And when we were on the point of fleeing, the Indians who held
us fought amongst themselves over a woman, and they punched each other
and struck one another with sticks and wounded one another in the head.
And with the great rage they felt, each one took his house and went off by
himself, whereupon it was necessary for all of us Christians who were there
also to part company, and by no means were we able to reunite until the
following year.[7] And during this time I endured a very bad life, as much
because of my great hunger as because of the bad treatment I received from
the Indians, which was such that I had to flee three times

1. Cabeza de Vaca was the first
European to give an account
of the American bison (*Bison
bison*). Oviedo does not record
Cabeza de Vaca's sighting of
bison on the Texas coast; the
first reference to bison in his
account pertains to the region
north of La Junta de los Ríos in
southwestern Texas (608a).

2. Castile.

3. Cabeza de Vaca evidently
drew on his exposure to the
bison along his entire journey
for this account; the people
who harvested the many hides
were evidently not the coastal
Indians but rather ones the
men encountered on their
overland journey.

4. Cabeza de Vaca's third
mention of the waiting period
during the spring and summer
of 1533.

5. Where the pecans were
eaten at the confluence of the
San Antonio and Guadalupe
Rivers.

6. In the area of Corpus Christi
Bay and south of the Nueces
River from the coast inland.
Oviedo (601a) states that the
prickly pears were located forty
leagues away in the direction
of Pánuco and that the Indians
followed along the coast until
they left the salt water and went
inland eating prickly pears.

7. The men were separated
at the end of the prickly pear

season (late summer) in 1533
and were forced to wait until
the end of the season of 1534 to
escape.

from the masters who held me, and they all went looking for me and put forth great effort to find and kill me.[1] And God our Lord in his mercy chose to preserve and protect me from them. And when the time of the prickly pears returned,[2] we again gathered in that same place. Inasmuch as we had resolved to flee and had set the day to do so, that same day the Indians separated us, and each one of us went his own way. And I said to my companions that I would wait for them at the prickly pear grounds until the moon was full. And this day was the first of September, and the first day of the new moon.[3] And I informed them that if they did not come during this time as we agreed, I would go alone and leave them behind. And thus we parted, and each one went off with his Indians. And I was with mine until the thirteenth day of the moon, and I had resolved to flee to other Indians on the full moon. And on the thirteenth day of the month, Andrés Dorantes and Estevanico arrived to where I was, and they told me how they had left Castillo with other Indians who were called Eanagados,[b] and that they were near there, and that they had endured great hardship, and that they had been wandering lost.[4] And the following day our Indians moved toward where Castillo was, and they went to join those who held him and make friends with one another, because up to that point they had been at war, and in this manner we recovered Castillo. During the entire time we ate the prickly pears we suffered thirst, and to remedy this we drank the juice of the prickly pears, and we extracted it and drew it out of a hole that we had made in the ground, and once it was full, we drank from it until we were satisfied. It is sweet and the color of

b. Eanagados] V: Anagados

1. In the spring of 1533, Cabeza de Vaca had been given to some relatives of the Mariames who were holding Dorantes (f29v).

2. Late summer 1534.

3. Cabeza de Vaca's references to specific dates six years after losing contact with Spanish civilization cannot be taken literally.

4. Using Dorantes's testimony from the Joint Report, Oviedo (601b–02b) offers an account of what happened to the three others up to the time of their reunion with Cabeza de Vaca.

boiled must.[1] They do this because they lack other vessels. There are many kinds of prickly pears, and among them some are very good, although all of them seemed to me to be so, and my hunger never permitted me to choose among them or to consider which were the best. The majority of these peoples drink rainwater collected in certain places because, even though there are rivers, since they are never permanently settled, they never have a known or fixed source of water. Throughout the land there are many and very beautiful grazing lands and good pastures for cattle, and it seems to me that it would be very productive land if it were worked and inhabited by men of reason.[2] We saw no mountains in any part of it that we had seen. Those Indians[3] told us that there were others farther ahead, called Camones, who live toward the coast, and they had killed all the men who came on the raft of Peñalosa and Téllez, and that they came so weakened, that although they were killing them, they did not defend themselves, and thus all of them perished.[4] And they showed us their clothes and weapons, and said that the raft was capsized there. This is the fifth raft to be accounted for, because the governor's had been carried out to sea, as we have said.[5] And that of the comptroller and the friars had been seen overturned along the coast, and Esquivel reported their fate.[6] About the two in which Castillo and I and Dorantes were traveling, we have already said that they sank next to the island of Malhado.[7]

[a]After having moved, two days later we commended ourselves to God our Lord, and we left fleeing,[8] trusting in the fact that although it was already late and the prickly pear season was ending,[9] with the

a.] Z: *om.* V: Chapter twenty: Of how we fled.

1. *arrope.* Must (*mosto*) is the expressed juice of fruit and especially of grapes before and during fermentation. *Arrope*, a Spanish term derived from Arabic, was used in the sixteenth century to describe a grape syrup produced by evaporating the juice to one third its original volume or to refer to a new sweet wine (Covarrubias 153a, 816a).

2. *gente de razón.* Euphemistically, Christians. See (f7v).

3. Throughout this section Cabeza de Vaca does not state the name of the Indian groups with which he was living from the time he left the Mariames until the four men reached the Avavares. This reference may refer to the Eanagados, with whom Dorantes and Estevanico had left Castillo, or to the Indians with whom they had found Cabeza de Vaca, whom he does not identify.

4. This last of the five rafts, pertaining to Téllez and Peñalosa, probably landed somewhere on Padre Island in mid-November 1528.

5. See (f30v).

6. See (f29v, f30v).

7. See (f21v, f23v).

8. This point does not mark the beginning of the men's continuous overland journey to México-Tenochtitlán. On the same day that the men fled from the Eanagados and the Indians with whom Cabeza de Vaca was staying, they encountered the Avavares in the prickly pear region. They would remain with them in the area north of the Rio Grande from the end of the prickly pear season of 1534 until the beginning of the season the following year.

9. September or October 1534.

fruits that remained in the countryside, we could travel a considerable distance. Pursuing our course that day with great fear that the Indians would follow us, we saw some spires of smoke. And going toward them, after vespers we arrived there, where we saw an Indian who, as he saw that we were coming toward him, fled without wanting to wait for us. We sent the black man after him. And since he saw that he was coming alone, he waited for him. The black man told him that we were going to look for those people who were making those spires of smoke. He responded that the houses were near there, and that he would guide us there. And thus we went following him. And he ran on ahead to give notice that we were coming. And at sunset we saw the houses. And at a distance of two crossbow shots before we came upon them, we found four Indians who were waiting for us, and they received us well. We told them in the language of the Mareames that we were coming to look for them. And they showed that they were pleased with our company, and thus they took us to their houses. And they lodged Dorantes and the black man in the house of a physician, and Castillo and me in that of others.[c] These people have another language, and they are called Avavares, and they are the ones who customarily took bows to our Indians and went to trade with them.[1] And although they are of another nation[2] and language, they understand the language of the ones we were with previously. And that same day they had arrived there with their houses. Later the people offered us many prickly pears, because they already had news of us and about how we were curing and about the wonders that our Lord was working through us, which although there should be no others, were truly great, opening roads for us through a land so deserted, bringing us people where many times

c. others] V: another

1. The Avavares were mentioned earlier (f29v). The prickly pear grounds where the men encountered them seem to have marked the northern extreme of this group's migratory range.

2. *nación.* A community of people of the same ethnic origin, generally sharing the same language and a common cultural tradition (DRAE 909a). Covarrubias (823a) uses *nación* in this sense when he refers to the Spanish people as "la nación española."

there were none, and liberating us from so many dangers and not permitting us to be killed, and sustaining us through so much hunger, and inspiring these people to treat us well, as we will describe later.

ªThat same night that we arrived, some Indians came to Castillo and said to him that they suffered a malady of the head, begging him to cure them. And after he had made the sign of the cross over them and commended them to God, at that point the Indians said that all the sickness had left them. And they went to their houses and brought many prickly pears and a piece of venison, a thing that we could not identify. And when this news was spread among them, many other sick people came that night to be cured. And each one brought a piece of venison. And there were so many of them that we did not know where to put the meat. We gave great thanks to God because each day his mercy and blessings were increasing. And after the cures were completed, they began to dance and make their *areitos* and celebrations, which lasted until sunrise of the following day. And the celebration held on account of our arrival lasted for three days. And at the end of them, we asked them about the land that lay ahead, and about the people that we would find in it, and the sources of food that were in it. They responded to us that throughout that entire land there were many prickly pears, but that the season was already over, and that there were no people because they had all gone to their homes, having already collected the prickly pears, and that the land was very cold and in it there were very few hides. Seeing that winter and cold weather were already upon us, we decided to spend it with these Indians.[1] Five days after we

1. Oviedo (602b–03a) remarks that from October (1534) until August of the following year the Christians lived in complete freedom among the Avavares, although they suffered great hunger and ate nothing but roots. He says they overwintered with them because they needed to collect hides with which to cover themselves on the journey ahead.

had arrived there, they left to hunt for other prickly pears where there were other people of different nations and tongues. And traveling five days with very great hunger because there were no prickly pears nor any other fruit along the route, we arrived at a river where we put up our houses.[1] And after setting them up, we went to look for the fruit of some trees, which is like [the fruit of] a vetch.[2] And since through all this land there are no trails, I stopped to investigate it more fully; the people returned and I remained alone, and going to look for them, that night I got lost. And it pleased God that I found a tree aflame, and warmed by its fire I endured the cold that night, and in the morning I gathered a load of firewood, and I took two firebrands and again looked for the people. And I continued in this manner for five days, always with my lighted torch and load of wood, so that if my fire died in a place where there was no firewood (since in many areas there was none), I would have the means to make other firebrands and I would not remain without a light, because against the cold I had no other recourse since I went naked as I was born. And for the night I had this defense, that is, I went to the groves of the wood near the rivers, and stopped in them before sunset. And in the earth I dug a pit with the butt of a timber[d3] and in it I threw a great deal of firewood from the trees that grow in great quantity there. And I gathered much dry wood fallen from the trees, and around that pit I placed four fires like the points of a cross. And I made an effort and took care to rekindle the fire from time to time, and from the long grass that grows there I made some bundles to cover myself in

d. with the butt of a timber]
V: *om.*

1. There is insufficient evidence to identify this river or the ones where Cabeza de Vaca says that he collected firewood and was lost. The Avavares seem to have migrated over an area somewhat inland but not completely isolated from the seacoast, between the Nueces River and the Rio Grande.

2. *yeros* (*hierros*, *hieros* in the Zamora [1542] edition). Coopwood (129) and Campbell and Campbell (26) identify this as the Texas ebony; Cabeza de Vaca's description is not specific enough, however, to determine that this was not simply his first reference to mesquite. See (f40r).

3. *coçe* (archaic for *coz*). Lowest or thickest part of a tree or timber (DRAE 375c).

that hole. And in this way I protected myself from the cold of night. And during one of them, the fire fell on the grass with which I was covered. And while I was sleeping in the pit the fire began to burn fiercely, and despite the great haste that I made to get out, my hair nevertheless received the sign of the danger in which I had been. In this entire time I did not eat a mouthful of food, nor did I find anything that I could eat, and since my feet were bare, they bled a great deal. And God took pity upon me, that in all this time the north wind did not blow, because otherwise it would have been impossible for me to survive. And at the end of five days, I arrived at a bank of a river where I found my Indians, for they and the Christians had already taken me for dead, and they were convinced that some viper had bitten me. All took great pleasure in seeing me, especially the Christians, and they told me that until then, they had traveled with great hunger, that this was the reason they had not searched for me, and that night they gave me to eat some of the prickly pears they had. And the next day we departed from there and went to where we found many prickly pears with which all satisfied their great hunger.[1] And we gave many thanks to our Lord because his succor never failed us.

^c^The next morning many Indians came there, and they brought five sick people who were crippled and very ill, and they came in search of Castillo, so that he could cure them. And each one of the sick people offered their bow and arrows. And he accepted them, and at sunset he made the sign of the cross over them and entrusted them to God our Lord and we all

c.] Z: *om.* V: Chapter twenty-two: How they brought us other sick people the next day.

1. This second region of prickly pears was slightly north of the Rio Grande.

a. we might bring] V: God send

prayed in the best way we could that we might bring[a] them health, since he saw that there was no other means by which to make those people help us so that we could leave so miserable a life. And he did it so mercifully that, come the morning, they all awoke so fit and healthy, and they went away as vigorously as if they had never had any malady whatsoever. This caused very great wonder among them, and it moved us to give many thanks to our Lord and to experience more fully his mercy, and to maintain firm the hope that he would deliver us and take us to where we could serve him. And for

c. complete] V: *om.*

myself I can say that I always had complete[c] faith in his mercy that he would deliver me from that captivity. And so I always said to my companions. Since the Indians had gone and taken away their ill ones now restored to health, we departed to where others were eating prickly pears. And these

d. Cuthalchuches] V: Cutalches

are called Cuthalchuches[d] and Malicones, which are other languages. And together with them there were others who were called Coayos and Susolas, and from another area, others called Atayos; and these were at war with the Susolas, and they shot arrows at each other every day. And since throughout the land nothing was talked about except the mysteries that God our Lord worked through us, people came from many places to seek us out so that we could cure them. And two days after they arrived there, some Indians of the Susolas came to us, and they begged Castillo to go and cure a wounded man and other sick people, and they said that among them there was one who was very near his end. Castillo was a very cautious physician, particularly when the cures were threatening and dangerous. And he believed that his sins would prevent the cures from turning out well every time. The Indians[1] told me that I should go to cure them because they held me in esteem, and they remembered that I had cured them at the nut-gathering grounds, and because of that, they had given us nuts and hides, and this had happened when I came to join the Christians.[2] And thus I had to go with them, and Dorantes and Estevanico went with me. And when I arrived near their huts, I saw the sick man whom we were going to cure, who was dead, because there were many people around him weeping and his house was undone, which is the sign that the owner is dead. And thus when I arrived, I found the Indian, his eyes rolled back in his head, and without any pulse, and with all the signs of death; so it seemed to me, and Dorantes said the same. I removed a mat that he had on top of him, with which he was covered. And as best I could, I beseeched our Lord to be served by giving health to that man and to all the others among them who were in need. And after having made the sign of the cross and blown on him many times, they brought me his bow and they gave it to me along with a basket of crushed prickly pears. And they took me to cure many others who had sleeping sickness,[3] and they gave me two other baskets of prickly pears, which I gave to our Indians[4] who had come with us. And having done this, we returned to our lodgings. And our Indians, to whom I had given the prickly pears, remained there, and at nighttime they returned to their houses and said that that one who had been dead and whom I had cured in their presence had arisen revived and walked about and eaten and spoken with them, and that as many as I had cured had become well and were without fever and[e] very happy.[5] This

e. without fever and] V: *om.*

1. Susolas.

2. The reference ostensibly suggests that the Susolas followed an annual migration route that extended, north to south, from the San Antonio and Guadalupe Rivers, where they ate pecans, to the prickly pear grounds near the Nueces River, to the southern prickly pear region near the northern bank of the Rio Grande, where they spent the winter. The curing episode would have taken place during the spring of 1533 (see f41v).

3. *modorra.* A sickness that makes its victim unconscious (Covarrubias 809a).

4. Avavares.

5. Cabeza de Vaca and his companions might not have been perceived as great shamans because they performed cures but rather performed cures because they were taken to be great shamans. Lévi-Strauss (173–75) theorizes that group expectation is a critical element in the shamanic complex, that is, the relations between the shaman, the sick person, and the community, organized around the poles of the intimate experience of the shaman on one extreme and group consensus on the other.

c. Culthalcuches] V: Cu-
talchiches

caused very great wonder and fear, and in all the land they spoke of nothing else. All those to whom this report arrived came looking for us so that we could cure them and make the sign of the cross over their children. And when the Indians who were in the company of ours, who were the Culthalcuches,[c] had to return to their land,[1] before leaving, they offered us all the prickly pears that they had gathered for their journey without keeping even one for themselves. And they gave us flints as long as a span and a half,[2] which they use for cutting, and it is an object of very great esteem among them. They beseeched us to remember them and to ask God to always keep them well, and we promised them that we would do so, and with this they departed the most contented people in the world, having given us all the best things they had. We were with those Avavares Indians eight months. And this reckoning we made by the moon.[3] In all this time people came from many areas looking for us. And they said that truly we were children of the sun.[4] Until then Dorantes and the black man had not performed any cures, but on account of the great demands made on us, [the Indians] coming from many places to look for us, we all became physicians, although in boldness and daring to perform any cure I was the most notable among them.[5] And we never cured anyone who did not say that he was better, and they had so much confidence that they would be cured if we performed the cures, that they believed that as long as we were there, none of them would die. These and the rest whom we had left behind told us something very strange, and by the explanation they put together for us,

1. The four Narváez survivors were with the Avavares; the Cuthalchuches were departing.

2. See (f13r).

3. From September or October 1534 to midsummer 1535. Cabeza de Vaca's calculation of the eight months spent with the Avavares according to the lunar cycle suggests that his calculations of the months, not to mention specific dates, were at best approximations.

4. The Narváez men understood the Indians to refer to indigenous beliefs about solar deities and their association of the Spaniards with them. Elsewhere Cabeza de Vaca (f48r) remarks that the Indians used this ruse in order to dupe one another about the four Narváez survivors.

5. See (f38r, f41v).

it seemed that it had occurred some fifteen or sixteen years earlier;[1] that they said that through that land went a man they call an evil being,[2] and that he was small in body and that he had a beard, although they were never able to see his face clearly, and that when he came to the house where they were, their hair stood on end and they trembled, and afterward he appeared at the door of the house with a flaming firebrand. And later that man came in and took whichever one of them he wanted, and he gave them three large incisions in the sides with a very sharp flint, a hand wide and two spans long.[3] And he placed his hand into those wounds and pulled out their entrails, and that he cut off a piece, more or less a span long, and threw the part that he cut off into the fire, and afterward he made three cuts in the arm, and the second one he made in the crook of the arm,[4] and dislocated it. And a little while afterward, he set it back into place, and he placed his hands over the wounds, and they told us that later they were healed, and that many times when they danced, he appeared among them, sometimes in the costume of a woman, and other times dressed as a man, and when he wanted, he picked up the *buhío*, or house, and raised it into the air, and a little while afterward he dropped it and it fell with a great blow. They also told us that many times they gave him food to eat and that he never ate anything, and that they asked him where he came from and where he had his house, and he showed them a cleft in the earth and said that his house was there below. We laughed a great deal about these things they told us, making fun of them. And since they saw that we did not believe them,

1. About 1518 or 1519.

2. *mala cosa.* In anthropological terms, the trickster, that is, the figure of the creator and destroyer without reference to divinity. The trickster is considered to be one of the most ancient expressions of humanity. His earliest forms are found among the natives of North America, and he is characterized by isolation from society and sexual transformation (Radin xxiii, 132–37). *Mala cosa* seems to replicate these traits.

3. See (f13r).

4. *sangradura.* The bend of the arm opposite the elbow (DRAE 1177b).

they brought many of those who said that he had taken them, and we saw the scars of the cuts that he had made in the places and in the manner they had said. We told them that he was an evil person. And in the best manner that we could, we gave them to understand that, if they believed in God our Lord and were Christians like us, they would not be afraid of him, nor would he dare to come and do those things to them, and they could be assured that as long as we were in the land, he would not dare to appear in it. With this they were very pleased, and they lost a great deal of the fear they had. These Indians[1] told us that they had seen the Asturian and Figueroa with others who were ahead on the coast,[2] whom we called [the people] of the figs.[3] All these people did not know how to calculate the seasons either by the sun or the moon, nor do they have reckoning of the months and years, but they understand and know the differences between the times when the fruit comes to mature and when the fish die and the stars appear, in the observance of which they are very skilled and well practiced. With these Indians we were always well treated, although we had to dig up what we ate, and we carried our loads of water and wood. Their houses and foodstuffs are like those of the previous people, although they have much greater hunger, because they do not have maize or acorns or nuts. We always went about naked as they did, and at night we covered ourselves with deerskins. Of the eight months we spent with them, we suffered great hunger during six, for even fish are not obtainable there.[4] And at the end of this time,[5] the

1. Avavares.

2. In the region of southern Mustang Island or Padre Island. Figueroa and the Asturian had fled down the coast from the region of Matagorda and St. Joseph Islands in the spring of 1529. According to Oviedo (598b–99a), they had vowed not to stop until they either reached Pánuco or met their death (see f31v).

3. See (f44r).

4. Cabeza de Vaca's remark about the lack of fish, also mentioned by Oviedo (602b), has led commentators to suppose that the Avavares lived considerably inland. The fact that the Avavares identified the time of year according to the availability of fish and that they provided information about the raft of Téllez and Peñalosa reveals that their zone of habitation was not far from the coast.

5. Midsummer 1535.

prickly pears were beginning to mature, and without our being perceived by them, we went to others who were ahead,[1] called Maliacones.[2] These Indians were a day's journey from where I and the black man arrived. At the end of three days, I sent him to bring over Castillo and Dorantes. And having come, we departed all together with the Indians who were going to eat a small fruit from some trees,[3] on which they sustain themselves during ten or twelve days before the prickly pears ripen. And there they met with these other Indians who are called Arbadaos, and we found these Indians to be very sick and emaciated and bloated, so much so that we were astonished, and the Indians with whom we had come returned by the same route. And we told them [the Maliacones] that we wanted to remain with those [others, the Arbadaos], about which they showed sorrow, and thus we remained in the countryside with those Indians near those houses. And when they saw us, they met together after having spoken among themselves, and each one of them took his own [Christian] by the hand and took us to their houses. With these people[4] we suffered more hunger than with the others, because in the entire day we ate nothing more than two fistfuls of that fruit, which was green; it had so much milk that it burned our mouths. And there being a lack of water, it produced great thirst in whomever ate it. And as our hunger was so great, we bought two dogs from them, and in exchange for them we gave them some nets and other things and a deerskin with which I covered myself.[5] I have already said how, throughout this entire land, we went about naked, and since we were not accustomed to it, like serpents we changed

---

1. This flight from the Avavares in midsummer 1535 (not the flight to them in late summer 1534) marks the beginning of the journey that led the four Christians back to Spanish civilization. See (f35r).

2. Sometime in midsummer 1535, when the prickly pears were first beginning to ripen. The date of the four men's departure from the Avavares to the Maliacones, whom they had first encountered the previous summer (f37v), is uncertain. Dates from May (eight months after their arrival at the Avavares), as stated by Cabeza de Vaca (f38v, f39v), to August (Oviedo 603a) 1535 have been proposed.

3. Mesquite (*Prosopis juliflora*). See (f45r–v).

4. Arbadaos.

5. Cabeza de Vaca here commences a digression (f40r–f41r) on the men's experiences from the Avavares Indians to the Arbadaos.

our skins twice a year. And with the sun and wind, there appeared on our chests and backs some very great ulcerations, which caused us very great distress on account of the large loads we carried, which were very heavy and caused the ropes to cut into the flesh of our arms. And the land is so rugged and impassable that many times when we gathered firewood in the dense thickets, when we finished taking it out we were bleeding in many places from the thorns and brambles that we encountered, for wherever they ensnared us they broke our skin. Sometimes it happened to me that, after shedding much blood in gathering wood, I could not haul it out, either on my back or by dragging it. I did not have, when I saw myself in these difficulties, any other remedy or consolation but to think about the Passion of our Redeemer Jesus Christ and the blood he shed for me, and to consider how much greater had been the torment that he suffered from the thorns, than that which I had to endure at that time. I traded with these Indians[1] by making combs for them, and with bows and arrows and nets. We made mats, which are objects of which they have great need. And although they know how to make them, they do not want to occupy themselves in any of it because of the need at the same time to search for food. And when they devote themselves to this they suffer very great hunger. On other occasions they ordered me to scrape hides and soften them. And the greatest prosperity in which I found myself there was the day they gave me a hide to scrape, because I scraped it very clean and ate of those scrapings, and that sufficed me for two or three days. It also happened to us, with these Indians and with the ones whom we

1. Avavares.

left behind, that we were given a piece of meat to eat raw. And if we put it to roast, the first Indian who came along carried it off and ate it. It seemed to us unwise to put it at such risk, and besides, we were not such that it troubled us to eat it roasted, but neither were we able to swallow it raw.[1] This is the life that we had there, and the little sustenance we obtained was through the objects of exchange that we made with our own hands.

[c]After we ate the dogs,[2] it seeming to us that we had the strength to be able to go on ahead, commending ourselves to God our Lord to guide us, we took leave of those Indians.[3] And they guided us to others of their language who were near there.[4] And pursuing our course, it rained that entire day and we walked in water. And in addition to this we lost our way, and we came to rest in a very great woods. And we gathered many prickly pear leaves and we cooked them that night in an oven we made, and we gave them so much flame that in the morning they were ready to eat. And after having eaten them, we entrusted ourselves to God, and we departed and found the path that we had lost. Beyond the woods, we found other houses of Indians. And when we arrived there, we saw two women and boys who became frightened as they walked through the thicket, and upon seeing us, they fled from us and went to alert the Indians who were going through the woods. And having approached, they stopped to watch us from behind some trees, and we called to them, and they came toward us with great fear.

c.] Z: *om.* V: Chapter twenty-three: How we departed after having eaten the dogs.

1. The Spanish text is ambiguous. The statement can be interpreted as a commentary on either the four men's cultural attitude toward eating raw meat or their physical capability to do so. We have elected the first interpretation, that the text implies a comparison between the cultural norms of the natives and the four Narváez survivors with respect to the consumption of raw flesh, suggesting that the natives were opposed to the four men cooking the meat and most likely did not understand the reason for doing so, because they perhaps thought that to cook the meat was to destroy it or render it inedible. Since the natives would carry off partially cooked meat and eat it, it seems most plausible that

their interest was in making the best use of the meat given its scarcity, and they probably thought that when the men cooked the meat they were wasting it. Smith (*Relation* 127) misinterprets the statement, insisting that the four Narváez survivors preferred raw meat to cooked.

2. Cabeza de Vaca here returns to the narrative of the four survivors' journey at their departure from the Arbadaos after the digression mentioned above (f40r).

3. Arbadaos.

4. The Arbadaos are the last group of natives that Cabeza de Vaca identifies by name. Some commentators have suggested that the inhabitants of the settlement of fifty houses that the men reached shortly after

leaving the Arbadaos were the Cuchendados, since this is the last group to which Cabeza de Vaca refers in his summary of the Indian groups (f44r).

And after having spoken to them, they told us that they had great hunger, and that near there were many of their own houses. And they said that they would take us to them. And that night we arrived to where there were fifty houses, and they were astonished to see us, and they showed great fear.[1] And after they were somewhat calmed about our presence, they came to us, placing their hands on our faces and bodies, and afterward they passed their hands over their own faces and bodies. And thus we remained that night, and come the morning they brought us the sick people they had, begging us to make the sign of the cross over them, and they gave us of what they had to eat, which were prickly pear leaves and cooked green prickly pears.[2] And because of the good treatment they gave us, and because they gave to us gladly and willingly what they had and were pleased to remain without food in order to give it to us, we stayed with them for some days.[3] And being there, others came from farther ahead.[4] When they were preparing to leave, we said to the first ones that we wanted to go with those others. It saddened them very much. And they entreated us earnestly not to go. And in the end we took leave of them, and we left them weeping because of our departure, because it grieved them profoundly.

[f]From the island of Malhado to this land[5] all the Indians whom we saw have as a custom, from the day their wives know they are pregnant, not to sleep with them until after two years of nurturing their children, who suckle until they are twelve years old, at which time they are of an age that by

f.] Z: *om.* V: Chapter twenty-four: Of the customs of the Indians of that land.

1. Oviedo (603b) declares that this was the very first occasion on which the natives "began to fear and show reverence for these few Christians and to esteem them highly." Cabeza de Vaca had attributed the beginning of the Indians' reverential conduct toward the men earlier, upon their arrival at the Avavares (f35v).

2. In Oviedo's (603b) account this is the first episode of curing. He compares the Narváez men's manner of curing to that of *saludadores*, or curers, in Castile, that is, by blessing and breathing upon the patient. Covarrubias (923b) defines this type of healer as one who cures by grace, *gratis data*, curing men of madness and restoring livestock to health. Covarrubias remarked that such individuals should be called "salivadores" instead of "saludadores" because they used their own saliva as an agent in curing.

3. According to Oviedo (603b), the men remained with these Indians for two weeks (fifteen days) and departed as the prickly pears were beginning to ripen.

4. From this point on, Cabeza de Vaca identifies no previously unmentioned native group by name.

5. Cabeza de Vaca here again interrupts the narration of the men's journey to summarize his observations of the customs of the peoples encountered, this time from Malhado to near the Rio Grande (f41v–f45r).

themselves they know how to search for food. We asked them why they raised them in this manner, and they said that because of the great hunger in the land it happened many times, as we had seen, that they went two or three days without eating, and sometimes four; and for this reason, they let their children suckle so that in times of hunger they would not die, since even if some should survive [without it], they would end up sickly and of little strength. And if by chance it happens that some fall ill, they leave them to die in those fields if it is not a child of their own,[1] and all the rest, if they cannot go with them, remain, but in order to transport a child or a sibling,[2] they carry them and bear them on their backs. All these men are accustomed to leaving their wives when there is disagreement between them, and they marry again whomever they please; this occurs among the childless men, but those who have children remain with their wives and do not leave them. And when in some villages they fight and have disputes with one another, they strike and club each other until they are worn out, and then they separate. Sometimes women separate them by going between them, since men do not intervene to separate them, and in spite of whatever passion grips them, they do not bring bows or arrows into it.[3] And as soon as they have fought with one another and settled the dispute, they take their houses and wives and go to live in the countryside, separated from the others until their rage has subsided. And as soon as they are calmed down and without anger, they return to their village. And henceforth they are friends, acting as if nothing had happened between them, nor is it necessary that anyone intervene to restore friendship, because this is the way they do it. And if those who are in conflict are not married, they go to others of their neighbors, and although they be their

1. *si no es hijo.* The Spanish is ambiguous, referring either to the practice of abandoning any infant not of one's own flesh (as we have here translated) or of abandoning female children. The Mariames and the Yguases are described (f31v–f32r) as the only groups who practiced female infanticide.

2. *un hijo o hermano.* The same ambiguity in the Spanish applies, as noted above.

3. Among the groups of this coastal area, women are described not only as mediators of intertribal conflict but also as conduits of travel and exchange. The first mention of such activity in this area was the passage of Cabeza de Vaca and Lope de Oviedo from Malhado to the pecan region of the San Antonio and Guadalupe Rivers, on which Deaguanes women served as guides (f28v). Similar patterns were repeated in subsequent cultural and geographic areas (f43r, f45v, f48r, f51v, f52v).

enemies, they receive them well and are pleased with them and give them of what they have, in such a manner that, when their anger has passed, they return to their village, coming back rich. They are all warlike people, and they have as much cunning to protect themselves from their enemies as they would have if they had been raised in Italy and in continuous war.[1] When they are in a place where their enemies can attack them, they set up their houses at the edge of the most rugged woods and of the greatest density they find there. And next to it they make a trench and sleep in it. All the warriors are covered with light brush, and they make their arrows. And they are so well covered and hidden that even if their heads are uncovered, they are not seen. And they make a very narrow path and enter into the middle of the woods. And there they make a place for their women and children to sleep. And when night comes, they light fires in their houses, so that if there should be spies, they would believe that they are in them. And before dawn, they again light the same fires, and if by chance their enemies come to attack the houses themselves, those who are in the trench surprise them and from the trenches do them much harm without those outside seeing them or being able to find them. And when there are no woods in which they can hide themselves in this manner and prepare their ambushes, they set up camp on the plain in the area that seems best to them. And they surround themselves with trenches covered with light brush and make their arrows with which they shoot the Indians, and these defenses they make for nighttime. While I was with the ones of Aguenes,[2] they not being warned, their enemies[3] came at midnight and attacked them and killed three of them and wounded many others, with the

1. A brief allusion to Cabeza de Vaca's military service in Italy in 1511–12 and the wars between France and Spain that occurred in Italy during his lifetime.

2. *De Aguenes.* A variant of Deaguanes (f28v).

3. Quevenes.

result that they fled from their houses forward through the woods. And as soon as they perceived that the others had gone, they returned to them. And they gathered up all the arrows that the others had shot at them, and as secretly as they could, they followed them and were near their houses that night without being perceived. And in the early morning[1] they attacked them and they killed five of them and injured many others, and made them flee and leave their houses and their bows with all their possessions. And a little while later the women of the ones who were called Quevenes came and negotiated between them and made them friends, although sometimes the women are the cause of war.[2] All these peoples, when they have particular enmities that are not among family members, kill each other at night by ambush and perform on one another great acts of cruelty.

c.] Z: *om.* V: Chapter twenty-five: How the Indians are quick with a weapon.

[c]These are the people most fit for war of all I have seen in the world, because if they are afraid of their enemies, all night they keep vigil with their bows at their sides and a dozen arrows, and the one who is sleeping checks his bow and if he finds it unstrung, he gives it the turns that are needed. Many times they go out of their houses crouched low to the ground so that they cannot be seen, and they watch and keep vigil all around to discover what is there. And if they sense something, in a moment they are all on the field with their bows and arrows, and thus they are until daybreak, running from one place to another, wherever they see it is necessary or they think their enemies might be. When day comes, they again unstring their bows

1. *al cuarto del alba.* Cabeza de Vaca used the Spanish military reference to the last of the four periods of the night watch in order to indicate when this event occurred.

2. Cabeza de Vaca would have witnessed the battle between the Deaguanes and the Quevenes in the region of Matagorda Bay in the spring of 1533.

until they go out to hunt. The bowstrings are made from the nerves of deer. The manner in which they fight is low to the ground. And while they are shooting their arrows, they go talking and leaping about from place to place, avoiding the arrows of their enemies, so much so that in such places they manage to suffer very little harm. The Indians are more likely to make fun of crossbows and harquebuses because these weapons are ineffective against them in the flat, open areas where they roam free. They are good for enclosed areas and wetlands; but in all other areas, horses are what must be used to defeat them, and are what the Indians universally fear. Whoever might have to fight against them should be advised to prevent them from perceiving weakness or greed for what they have. And as long as war lasts, they must treat them very badly, because if they know that their enemy has fear or some sort of greed, they are the people who know how to recognize the times in which to take vengeance and they take advantage of the fear of their enemies. In war, when they have shot at one another and spent their ammunition, they return along their own route without following one another, although they be many and the others few, and this is their custom. Many times they are shot through and through by arrows, and they do not die of the wounds if they are not struck in the abdomen or the heart; instead they heal very quickly. They see and hear more and they have sharper senses than any other men that I think there are in the world. They are great sufferers of hunger and thirst and cold, as they are more accustomed and hardened to it than others. This I have wanted to tell because, beyond the fact that all men desire to know the customs and practices of others, the ones who sometime might come to confront them should be informed about their customs and stratagems, which tend to be of no small advantage in such cases.

[b]I also want to tell about the nations[1] and languages that are found from the island of Malhado to the last ones, who are Cuchendados.[c] On the island of Malhado there are two languages: some are called of Cavoques,[d] and the others, of Han. On the mainland in front of the island there are others who are called of Charruco,[e] and they take the name of the woods where they live. Ahead on the coast of the sea live others who are called the Deguenes,[f2] and in front of them, others who have as a name the ones of Mendica. Farther down the coast are the Quevenes, and in front of them on the mainland, the Mariames. And following forward along the coast are others who are called Guaycones, and facing these Indians, on the mainland, the Yeguazes.[g] Beyond these Indians are others who are called Atayos, and behind these others, Acubadaos, and of these there are many ahead along this route. On the coast live others called Quitoles, and in front of these Indians, on the mainland, the Chavavares.[i] With these join together the Maliacones, and others, the Cultalchulches,[j] and others who are called Susolas, and others who are called Comos. And ahead on the coast are the Camoles. And on the same coast farther along [are] others whom we call the people of the figs.[3] All these peoples have dwellings and villages and diverse languages. Among these Indians there is a language in which they call to a person saying for "look over here," "arraca,"[k] and to dogs, "xo." In the entire

b.] Z: *om.* V: Chapter twenty-six: Of the nations and languages.

c. who are Cuchendados] V: *om.*

d. Cavoques] V: Caoques

e. Charruco] V: Chorruco

f. the Deguenes] V: Doguenes

g. Yeguazes] V: Yguazes

i. Chavavares] V: Avavares

j. Cultalchulches] V: Cu-talchiches

k. arraca] V: arre aca

1. See (f35v).

2. Deaguanes.

3. The term "figs" pertains to prickly pears, and the prickly pear cactus came to be known as the "fig tree of the Indies." Although the general description "people of the figs" suggests "people of the prickly pears," it obviously refers to a specific Indian group or groups, rather than to all those who frequented the prickly pear grounds. See (f39v).

land they intoxicate themselves with something they smoke[1] and they give everything they have for it. They also drink another thing, which they extract from the leaves of trees like those of an oak,[2] and they toast it in certain vessels over the fire, and after they have it toasted, they fill the vessel with water, and thus they keep it over the fire, and when it has boiled twice, they pour it into a different vessel and they cool it with half a gourd. And when it has a great deal of foam, they drink it as hot as they can tolerate it. And from the time they take it out of the vessel until they drink it, they shout, saying, "Who wants to drink?" And when the women hear these shouts, they immediately stop without daring to move, and although they may be carrying heavy loads, they do not dare to do another thing. And if by chance one of them moves, they dishonor[3] her and beat her with sticks and with very great rage they pour out the water that they have [prepared] for drinking. And what they have drunk they disgorge, which they do very easily and without any trouble. They give a reason for this custom: and they say that if, when they desire to drink that water, the women move from where they are when they hear the voice, through that water something bad enters their bodies, and that a little while later it makes them die. And all the while the water cooks, the vessel must remain covered. And if by chance it is uncovered and some woman passes by, they pour it out and drink no more of that water. It is yellow, and they drink it for three days without eating. And each day each one of them drinks one and a half *arrobas*[4] of it. And when the women are menstruating[5] they do not search for food except for themselves, because no other person will eat what she brings. In the time that thus I was among these people,[6] I saw a

1. Although some commentators have identified this plant as tobacco or peyote, it is not possible to identify it given Cabeza de Vaca's lack of description.

2. This tree has been identified as a type of holly (genus *Ilex*)—the *Ilex cassine* by Hodge (88n1) and the *Ilex vomitiva* by Smith (*Relation* 139n3). Hodge describes the liquid prepared as a black tea; Cabeza de Vaca reported that the drink he saw was yellow. Again, the description is too vague to identify the plant.

3. *deshonrar*. A euphemism for rape. *Deshonra*, "the affront that removes one's honor" (Covarrubias 461a).

4. A weight of 25 pounds (11.5 kilograms). A measure of liquid that varies in weight according to the density of the liquid and the region where the measurement is used (Covarrubias 152a; DRAE 123c). A Spanish liquid measure, weighing 25 pounds and varying from 2.6 to 3.6 gallons in volume (*Simon and Schuster's* 955b).

5. *Están con su costumbre.* "Menstruation, in women, is called 'custom' because of being normal and habitual" (Covarrubias 366b).

6. The group in which Cabeza de Vaca encountered the men he describes here cannot be identified.

a. do not] V: *om.*

wicked behavior,[1] and it is that I saw one man married to another, and these are effeminate, impotent men. And they go about covered like women, and they perform the tasks of women, and they do not[a] use a bow, and they carry very great loads. And among these we saw many of them, thus unmanly as I say, and they are more muscular than other men and taller; they suffer very large loads.[2]

b.] Z: *om.* V: Chapter twenty-seven: Of how we moved on and were well received.

[b]After we departed from those whom we left weeping,[3] we went with the others to their houses. And we were well received by those who were in them, and they brought their children for us to touch with our hands, and they gave us much mesquite flour. This mesquite is a fruit that, when it is on the tree, is very bitter, and it is like carobs,[4] and it is eaten with earth and with it, it is sweet and good to eat. The manner in which they prepare it is as follows: they make a pit in the ground to the depth that they desire. And after throwing the fruit in this hole, they grind it with a timber as thick as a man's leg and a fathom[5] and a half long until it is very fine, and in addition to the earth that sticks to it from the hole, they bring [an amount equivalent to] a curry-combful[e6] and they throw it in the hole, and they grind it again a while longer, and afterward they pour it into a vessel that is like a two-handled basket. And they put in as much water as is necessary to cover it completely. And the one who has ground it tastes it, and if it seems to him that it is not sweet, he asks for more dirt and he mixes it with it. And he does this until he finds it sweet. And they all sit down around there, and each one puts his hand in and takes out what he can, and they again toss the pits and the pods of it onto some skins. And the one who has ground them

e. [an amount equivalent to] a curry-combful] V: more handfuls

1. *diablura.* Covarrubias's (468a) definition, under the entry *diablo* (devil), suggests a range of meaning from prankish to satanic.

2. To a limited degree these individuals correspond to the modern anthropological category of the berdache (see Angelino and Shedd; Schnarch).

3. Cabeza de Vaca here resumes the narration that he had previously interrupted (f41v).

4. *algarrovas.*

5. 5.5 feet (1.67 meters) (Hemming 518; DRAE 201b).

6. *almohazada.* According to Covarrubias (100b), the *almohaza* was "a curry-comb made of iron with three or four types of teeth with which horses and other animals were brushed, removing from them dirt and dead skin, and smoothing the hair." *Almohazada* probably referred to an estimated measure related to this instrument.

collects them and again tosses them into that basket and adds more water as he did previously, and again presses out the juice and water that comes from it, and he places the pits and pods again on the skin. And in this manner they do this grinding three or four times. And those who find themselves in this banquet, which for them is very great, end up with very swollen bellies from the earth and water that they have drunk. And from this the Indians made for us a very great celebration. And there were among them very great dances and *areitos* as long as we were there. And when we were sleeping at night, at the door of the dwelling where we were staying, six men kept watch with very great care over each one of us so that no one would dare to come inside until the sun had risen. When we wanted to leave them, some women of the others who lived ahead arrived there. And informed by them where those houses were, we departed for there, although they beseeched us greatly to remain there that day because the houses to which we were headed were far away, and there was no road in their direction. And [they said] that those women arrived tired, and resting another day, they would go with us and guide us, and thus we took our leave. And a little while later, the women who had come went after us with others from the same village. But since there were no trails through the land, we subsequently got lost, and thus we walked four leagues. And at the end of them we managed to drink at a watering place where we found the women who were following us, and they told us about the difficulty they had had in reaching us. We departed from there, taking them as guides. And we crossed a river[1] when it was already late

1. The Rio Grande, somewhere between its confluence with the Río San Juan and the coast of the Gulf of Mexico.

in the afternoon, which had water that came up to our chests; it was probably as wide as that of Seville,[1] and it ran very swiftly. And at sunset we arrived at a hundred houses of Indians, and before we arrived, all the people who were in them came out to receive us with so much shouting that it was a fright and vigorously slapping their thighs. They carried pierced gourds with stones inside, which is the item of highest celebration, and they do not take them out except to dance or to cure, nor does anyone but they dare to use them. And they say that those gourds have virtue and that they come from the sky,[2] because throughout that land there are none nor do they know where they might be, but only that the rivers bring them when they flood. So great was the fear and agitation that these people experienced that with some trying to arrive more quickly than others to touch us, they crowded us so much that they nearly could have killed us. And without letting our feet touch the ground, they carried us to their houses. And they fell so much[c] upon us and pressed us in such a manner that we went into the houses they had prepared for us. And we did not consent in any way to their making more celebrations with us that night. They spent that entire night dancing and performing *areitos* among themselves. And the next morning they brought us all the people of that village for us to touch and make the sign of the cross over them, as we had done to the others with whom we had been. And after this was done, they gave many arrows to the women of the other village who had come with theirs. The next day we left there, and all the people of the village went with us. And when we arrived at other Indians we were very[d] well

c. they fell so much] V: so many of them fell

d. very] V: *om.*

1. The Guadalquivir River (Oviedo 604a).

2. Here and later (f55v, f56v), Cabeza de Vaca reports the Indians' explanation for the origin of plants and people not indigenous to their area. In the phrase "vienen del cielo" the term *cielo*, understood to mean "sky," may be assigned cosmological significance, but not that of the sacred Christian concept of heaven that commentators since Oviedo and Las Casas have given it.

received as we had been by the previous ones. And thus they gave us some of the things they had and the deer they had killed that day. And among these people we saw a new custom, and it is that the ones who were with us took from those who came to be cured their bows and arrows and shoes and beads if they brought them. And after having taken them, they placed those people before us, so that we might cure them.[1] And once cured, they went away very content, saying that they were healed. Thus we departed from those Indians and we went to others by whom we were very well received, and they brought us their sick, who, on our making the sign of the cross over them, said that they were healed. And any one who did not improve believed that we could cure him.[2] And with what the others whom we cured told them, they made such merriment and dancing that they did not let us sleep. [b]Departing from these people, we went to many other houses, and at this point another new custom commenced, and it is that receiving us very well, those who came with us began to treat the others very badly, taking their possessions and sacking their houses without leaving them any single thing. About this we were much distressed to see the bad treatment that was given to those who thus received us, and also because we feared that that practice would be or would cause some altercation and scandal among them. But since we were powerless to remedy it or to dare to punish those who did it, for the time being we had to endure it until we had more authority among them. And also the same Indians who lost their households, on seeing our sadness, consoled us by saying that we should not be grieved by that, because they were so content to have seen us that they considered that

b.] Z: *om.* V: Chapter twenty-eight: Of another new custom.

1. Here begins a pattern of ritual pillage and exchange that was repeated many times over the course of this ten-month journey. Cabeza de Vaca explains that the practice needed to be taught to the inland-oriented groups with whom the Christians subsequently came into contact (f48r–v).

2. On the nature of the consensual relationship between shaman and patient, see (f38r).

their possessions had been well employed, and that farther ahead they would be compensated by others who were very rich. Along this entire road we had very great difficulty because of the many people who followed us. And we could not flee from them, although we tried, because the quickness with which they came to touch us was very great. And so great were their demands about this, that for three hours we could not finish with them so that they would leave us alone. The next day they brought us all the people of the village. And the majority of them are blind in one eye from a clouded spot that they have in it,[1] and others of them are completely blind because of them; about all this we were astonished. They are very well proportioned and of very good features, whiter than any others of all those we had seen up to that point. Here we began to see mountains,[2] and it seemed that they came in a chain from toward the North Sea.[3] And thus by the account that the Indians gave us about this, we believe that they are fifteen leagues from the sea. From here we departed with these Indians, heading toward these sierras to which we refer. And they took us to where some relatives of theirs were, because they did not want to take us except through where their relatives lived, and they did not want their enemies to obtain as much good as it seemed to them it would be to see us. And when we had arrived, those who came with us sacked the others. And since they knew the custom, before we arrived they hid some things. And after they had received us with great festivity and elation, they brought out what they had hidden and came to present it to us. And this was beads and red ocher and some little bags of silver.[4] According to our custom, we then gave it

1. *nube.* A film that develops in the eye (Covarrubias 831b); a small white film that forms on the cornea, obscuring sight such that light rays entering the eye seem to be passing through a cloud (DRAE 926a).

2. Mountains of Tamaulipas, most likely the chain of the Sierra de Pamoranes and the Sierra San Carlos farther south. On two occasions (f16r, f35r) prior to this first sighting, Cabeza de Vaca remarked on the absence of mountains in the coastal regions that they had traversed (in Florida and Texas). The reference to the mountains' proximity to the sea suggests that the men hoped that these mountains would be, or would merge into, the coastal range that extended from the Río de las Palmas to the Río Pánuco, their final destination.

3. The combined Atlantic Ocean, Caribbean Sea, and Gulf of Mexico. Here the immediate reference is to the Gulf of Mexico.

4. See (f49r).

to the Indians who had come with us, and when they had given it to us, they began their dances and fiestas and sent ahead to call others from another village that was near there so that those people could come to see us, and in the afternoon they all came and they brought us beads and bows and other little things that we also distributed. And the next day, when we were wanting to leave, all the people wanted to bring us to other friends of theirs who were at the near end of the sierras, and they said that there there were many houses and people, and that they would give us many things. But because this was off our route, we refused to go to them, and we took the course through the plain near the mountains, which we believed were not far from the coast.[1] All the people of the coast are very bad, and we considered it preferable to go through the land because the people farther inland are of a better disposition and they treated us better, and we considered it certain that we would find the land more populated and with better means of sustenance.[2] Finally, we did this because, by crossing through the land, we would see many of its particularities, because if God our Lord were served by taking some one of us out of there and bringing him to the land of Christians, he could give an account and description of it.[3] And since the Indians saw that we were determined not to go through the area where they led us, they told us that where we wanted to go there were no people, nor prickly pears, nor any other thing to eat. And they begged us to remain there that day, and thus we did so.[4] Later they sent two Indians to search for people along the road we wanted to pursue.[5] And the next day we departed, taking with

1. The Sierra de Pamoranes of northern Tamaulipas. The men still desired to travel southward toward Pánuco.

2. Cabeza de Vaca here implies that the men had improved their condition by moving slightly away from the coast to the Avavares and subsequent peoples. The men had undoubtedly hoped to find agricultural peoples, rather than more hunters and gatherers of the type with whom they had spent the previous seven years (1528–35) on or very near the seacoast.

3. This statement has been interpreted almost universally as a declaration of the party's decision to cross overland to the other sea. It represents instead the men's intention to travel somewhat inland and parallel to the coast rather than directly along it in their search for Pánuco. By doing so, they could potentially gather new data about the unknown inland areas north of the Río Pánuco rather than duplicate information about the coastal areas already available from Spanish maritime exploration of the Gulf of Mexico.

4. The Indians desired to take the four men into the mountains and to the coastal areas where they lived. The men sought to avoid both the rugged terrain, where they would be vulnerable to surprise attack, and the coastal groups, whom they expected to be hostile. Their immediate aim was to seek better sources of sustenance. At this point, the men had not yet abandoned their search for Pánuco; ultimately, however, they continued on a northwestward course until reaching western Mexico.

5. Inland, to Pánuco.

us many of them. And the women went carrying the water, and so great was
our authority among them that none dared to drink without our permission.
Two leagues from there we came upon the Indians who had gone to look
for the people, and they said that they had not found them, about which
the Indians showed sadness, and they again beseeched us to go through the
mountains.[1] We refused to do it, and since they saw our determination, they
bade us farewell, although with great sorrow, and they returned downriver
to their homes. And we traveled upstream.[2] And a little while later we came
upon two women encumbered, who, upon seeing us, stopped and put down
their loads and brought us some of what they were carrying, which was maize
flour, and they told us that farther ahead on that river we would find houses
and many prickly pears and more of that flour.[3] And thus we took leave of
them, because they were going to the others from whom we had departed.
And we walked until sunset.[4] And we arrived at a village of about twenty
houses where they received us weeping and with great sorrow because they
already knew that wherever we went all the people were sacked and robbed
by those who accompanied us. But since they saw us alone, they lost their
fear and gave us prickly pears and not another single thing. We stayed there
that night, and at dawn the Indians who had left us the previous day fell
upon their houses.[5] And since they took them unprepared and vulnerable,
they took from them all that they wanted without there being opportunity to
hide anything, about which they wept greatly. And the attackers, to console
them, told them that we were children of the sun,[6] and that we had the
power to cure the sick and to kill them and other lies even greater than
these, since they

1. The Sierra de Pamoranes of north-central Tamaulipas.

2. Somewhere on the San Lorenzo–Conchos–San Fernando river system in Tamaulipas, heading upstream and south-southwest on the Río San Fernando from a point downstream from its confluence with the Río Conchos, or going upstream on the Río Conchos from a spot downstream from its confluence with the Río San Lorenzo. Their eventual turn northwestward and passage from present-day Tamaulipas into Nuevo León can be explained by their following either river upstream to its point of confluence and taking the north-northwest-tending branch, that is, the Río Conchos or the Río San Lorenzo, respectively.

3. This account is absent from Oviedo's text. Given Cabeza de Vaca's need to justify a detour in the course toward Pánuco, he may have invented this incident in order to demonstrate that travel farther inland was the most prudent course in the men's search for food and their quest for survival. The men had not encountered maize since they had left the Florida Panhandle, and they would find no further evidence of it until they reached La Junta de los Ríos at the Texas-Chihuahua border (f52v).

4. This is virtually the last time the party traveled without Indian guides until the end of their journey.

5. The attacking Indians are those who had earlier stated that there were no people in this direction and whose scouts had said that they had found none (f47v; Oviedo 605b–06a).

6. See (f38v).

know how best to do it when they feel that it suits them. And they told them to lead us onward with great respect and to be careful not to anger us in anything, and to give us everything they had, and to try to take us where there were many people, and that wherever we arrived, to steal and loot what the others had, because such was the custom. ᶜAnd after having informed and instructed them well in what they were to do, they returned and left us with those Indians who, mindful of what the others had told them, began to treat us with that same fear and reverence that the others had. And we traveled with them for three days, and they took us to where there were many people. And before we arrived, they announced that we were coming and they told everything about us that the others had taught them and they added much more, because all these Indian peoples are very fond of tales and very deceitful, particularly when they are pursuing some gain. And when we arrived near the houses, all the people came out to receive us with great pleasure and festivity, and among other things, two of their physicians gave us two gourds.[1] And from this point forward we began to carry gourds with us, and we added to our authority this ceremony, which to them is very great. Those who had accompanied us sacked the houses, but since the houses were many and they were few, they could not carry everything they took, and they left more than half of it abandoned. And from here through the foothills of the sierra, we went inland more than fifty leagues,[2] and at the end of them we found

1. The four Narváez expedition survivors had recently come upon gourds for the first time. After crossing the Rio Grande, they encountered natives who used them ritually and indicated that they had obtained them as they came floating down the river (f46r). Cabeza de Vaca may have overlooked his earlier mention (f44v) of "half a gourd" used by the Indians of the area north of the Rio Grande to cool the intoxicating drink they prepared for consumption, or he may have considered the gourds (*calabazas*) used ceremonially to be of a different type. The men were still in Tamaulipas when they took up their own ceremonial use of the gourds.

2. North-northwest from the upper Río San Lorenzo through the low ranges of the Sierra de Cerralvo or west along the Río Conchos into the foothills of the Sierra Madre Oriental, passing from Tamaulipas into Nuevo León.

forty houses. And among other things that they gave us, they gave Andrés Dorantes a large, thick, copper bell,[1] and on it was outlined a face, and they showed that they valued it greatly. And they told them[2] that they had obtained it from other people who lived nearby. And asking them where those people had obtained them, they told them that they had brought it from toward the north, and that there was a great deal more of it there, and it was held in great esteem. And we understood that from wherever it had come, there was metalworking and that they worked it by casting.[3] And with this we departed the next day and we crossed a sierra of seven leagues,[4] and the stones in it were of iron slag.[5] And at night we arrived at many houses that were set up along the bank of a very beautiful river.[6] And the owners of them came halfway to meet us with their children on their backs, and they gave us many little bags of silver[d7] and others of powdered antimony;[8] with this they smear their faces. And they gave many beads and many hides of cows,[9] and they loaded all those who came with us with some of everything they had. They ate prickly pears and pine nuts,[10] and there are throughout that land[11] small pines, and the cones of them are like small eggs, but the pine nuts are better than those of Castile, because they have a very thin hull. And when they are green they grind them and make them into lumps and they eat them in this manner, and if they are dry they grind them with the hulls and they eat them as a powder. And those who received us there, as soon as they had touched us, turned running toward their houses. And then they returned to us, and they did not cease running back and forth. In this way they

d. silver] V: marcasite

1. Oviedo (606a) adds that these people also gave them cotton mantles, which also came from the north.

2. The Indians of this village of forty houses here explain the provenance of the copper bell not directly to the four men but to the Indians who accompanied them.

3. The evidence of cast metals to the north suggested a higher civilization than any the party had encountered since arriving on the Florida Peninsula.

4. Sierra de la Gloria, southeast of Monclova in present-day Coahuila.

5. *escoria*. The scoriaceous lava from a volcano or the dross or scoria of a metal (Covarrubias 539a).

6. Río Nadadores, north of Monclova, or one of its tributaries.

7. Probably marcasite. Oviedo (617b–18a) says in the chapter he wrote after reading Cabeza de Vaca's published *relación* that "plata" (silver) was a printer's error; his own text, however, reads "margarita" (margarite or pearl). This too is evidently an error in printing; Oviedo's text should have read "margaxita" (modern *margajita*), that is, marcasite (crystallized iron pyrites), which has a metallic appearance.

8. *alcohol* (Arabic *al-kuhl*, *kohl*), powder of antimony. A preparation of crushed antimony or galena used in Muslim and Asian countries, as well as in Europe, as a cosmetic around the eyes. Covarrubias (76a) describes it as a powder used to make the eyes sparkle and darken the eyelashes in order to make them beautiful.

9. See (f34r).

10. In English there is a distinction between the older "pine nut" (twelfth century), which is the edible seed of any of several pines, and "piñon," from the Spanish *piñón*, which is the edible seed of any of various low-growing pines (such as *Pinus cembroides*, *P. parryana*, *P. edulis*, and *P. monophylla*) of western North America, including Mexico.

11. Present-day Coahuila from the Monclova Basin northward; Cabeza de Vaca's reference may extend to the north of the Rio Grande, where the men also found piñon nuts in abundance.

brought us many things for our journey. Here they brought me a man, and they told me that a long time ago he had been wounded through the right shoulder with an arrow, and the point of the arrow rested over his heart. He said that it caused him much distress, and that for that reason he was always ill. I touched him and felt the point of the arrow, and I saw that it had passed through the cartilage.[1] And with a knife that I had, I opened his chest to that place. And I saw that the point had passed through and was very difficult to remove. I again cut deeper, and I inserted the knife point, and with great difficulty, at last I pulled it out. It was very long and, with a deer bone, plying my trade as a physician, I gave him two stitches.[a] And when I had removed the point, they asked me for it and I gave it to them. And the entire village came to see it, and they sent it through the land so that those who were there could see it. And on account of this they performed many dances and celebrations as they are accustomed to doing. And two days later,[b] I removed the two stitches from the Indian and he was healed.[c] And he said that he felt no pain or discomfort whatsoever. And this cure gave us a very great reputation among them throughout the whole land, to the degree that they were able and knew how to esteem and appreciate anything. We showed them that bell that we were carrying, and they told us that in the place from which it had come, there were many deposits of that material[2] in the ground, and that it was a thing they valued highly, and that there were permanent houses. And this we believe to be the South Sea since we always had notice that that sea is richer than the one of the North. We departed from these people[3] and we went through so many types of

a. stitches.] V: stitches, (and after they had been given) he bled a great deal and with a piece of shredded hide I stopped the bleeding.

b. two days later] V: the next day

c. healed.] V: healed, and the incision that I had made in him looked like nothing more than a crease in the palm of one's hand.

1. *ternilla.* Neither flesh nor bone but like the tissue of the nose and ears (Covarrubias 959a).

2. *planchas de aquello.* Here, copper sheets. *Plancha*: broad, thin sheets of metal, according to Covarrubias (873b).

3. The ones whom the men encountered along the beautiful river (Río Nadadores or a tributary of it) after crossing the Sierra de la Gloria and who had given them bison hides, cotton mantles, piñon nuts, and bags of marcasite and powdered antimony.

people and such diverse languages that memory is insufficient to be able to recount them.[1] And the ones always sacked the others, and thus those who lost, like those who gained, were very content. We carried so great a company that in no manner could we make use of them. In those valleys through which we passed each of them carried a club three spans long and all of them went in a row. And when a hare, of which there was an abundance there, jumped out, they surrounded it and fell upon it with so many clubs that it was a wonder to see. And in this manner they made it run from one to another, which in my opinion was the most beautiful type of hunting that one could imagine, because many times they came right up to their hands. And when at night we stopped, they had given us so many that each of us carried eight or ten loads of them. And those who carried bows did not go before us. Rather, they spread out over the sierra to hunt deer. And at night when they returned, they brought for each one of us five or six, and many[b] birds and quail and other game. Everything, finally, that the people[c] killed, they put before us without daring to take one single thing without our first making the sign of the cross over it, even though they might be dying of hunger, because thus they had it as a custom since traveling with us. And the women carried many mats of which they made houses for us, for each of us a separate one, with all his company.[2] And when this was done, we ordered that they roast those deer and rabbits and everything that they had taken. And this

b. six, and many] V: six deer and

c. Everything, finally, that the people] V: Finally, everything that that people found and

1. The party was heading north-northwest through the valleys of the north-northwest-tending sierras of northwestern Coahuila.

2. *con toda su gente conoscida.* Cabeza de Vaca suggests that each of the four travelers had a group of followers, including women, who associated exclusively with him.

also was done very quickly in some ovens that they made for the purpose. And we ate a little of all of it and the rest we gave to the lord of the people who went with us, ordering him to distribute it among them all.[1] Each one came to us with the portion assigned to him so that we might blow on it and make the sign of the cross over it because otherwise they would not dare to eat of it. And many times we brought with us three or four thousand people. And our labor was so great because we had to blow on and make the sign of the cross over what each of them was to eat and drink, and for many other things they wanted to do, they came to ask our permission, for which reason one can see how many importunities we entertained. The women brought us prickly pears and spiders and worms and whatever they could find, because, although they might be dying of hunger, they would eat nothing without our giving it to them. And going with these Indians, we crossed a great river[2] that flowed from the north. And after crossing some plains[3] of thirty leagues, we found many people who came to receive us from very far from there. And they came out to the road over which we were to travel and received us as the previous ones had.

[b]From here there was another manner of receiving us with regard to the sacking, because those who came out to the roads to bring us something for those who came with us were not robbed. Rather, after we had entered their houses, they themselves offered to us everything they had, and their houses with it. We gave them to the lords for them to distribute among the people. And those who remained dispossessed always

b.] Z: *om.* V: Chapter thirty: Of how the custom of receiving us changed.

1. The native lords were in charge of the distribution of these goods, which suggests that, despite Cabeza de Vaca's claims, the leadership of this entourage was not exclusively in the hands of the four men.

2. The Río Babía or its southern extension, the Río Sabinas, flowing from northwest to southeast across northern Coahuila.

3. High plateau area through which the lower Río Babía and the Río Sabinas pass, between that river system and the Rio Grande.

followed us, from which the number of people grew to compensate for their loss. And they told them that they should take care and not hide a single thing of whatever they had because it was impossible for us not to find out about it and later we would see to it that they all died.[a1] So great were the fears that they instilled in them that the first days they were with us, they were always trembling and did not dare to speak or raise their eyes to the heavens. These Indians guided us through more than fifty leagues of deserted land in very rugged sierras.[2] And because they were so dry there was no game in them, and because of this we suffered much hunger, and at the end [we crossed] a very great river[3] in which the water came up to our chests. And from here many of the people we brought began to fall ill from the great hunger and hardship they had suffered in those sierras, which were bitter and difficult in the extreme. These same ones took us to some plains at the end of the sierras, where they came to receive us from very far away from there.[4] And they welcomed us as the previous ones had done and gave so many things to those who came with us that, not being able to carry it, they left half of it. And we said to the Indians who had given it that they should reclaim and take it with them so that it not remain there abandoned. And they replied that by no means would they do so because it was not their custom, after having first offered it, to take it back again. And thus, holding it in low estimation, they let all of it be lost. To these Indians we said that we wanted to go to where the sun set.[5] And they replied to us that in that direction the people were far away. And we ordered them to send

1. The Valladolid (1555) edition adds the phrase "because the sun so commanded us," thus underscoring the notion that the Indians either took the four Narváez expedition survivors to be divine or used this ruse to intimidate potentially uncooperative victims (see f38v, f48r–v).

2. The uninhabited desert mountains of the Sierra Madre Oriental in Coahuila, in the area of the Arroyo de la Babía and northward to the Rio Grande.

3. This was their second crossing of the Rio Grande, somewhere along the northern border of present-day Coahuila, probably in the vicinity of Boquillas del Carmen or slightly farther northeast, into southwestern Texas.

4. The Stockton Plateau in southwestern Texas.

5. This clear notion of an itinerary is probably anachronistic; the party would only learn where to find maize (that is, to the west) after arriving at the permanent settlements at La Junta de los Ríos (f53v).

people to inform them that we were going there, and from this they excused themselves as best they could, because they were their enemies and they did not want us to go to them, but they did not dare to do anything else. And thus they sent two women, one of their own and another who was a captive of theirs. And they sent them out because women can mediate even when there is war.[1] And we followed them and stopped in a place where it was agreed that we would wait for them, but it took them five days to return. And the Indians said that they must not have found any people. We told them to lead us toward the north. They responded in the same manner, saying that in that direction there were only people very far away, and that there was nothing to eat nor was water to be found. And despite all of this, we insisted and said that we wanted to go there. And they still declined in the best way they could. And because of this we became angry. And I went one night to sleep in the countryside, apart from them,[2] but later they went to where I was. And they were there the entire night without sleeping and with very great fear and speaking to me and telling me how terrified they were, begging us to not be angry anymore, and that even though they knew they would die on the road, they would take us wherever we wanted to go. And as we still pretended to be angry, and because their fear did not subside, a strange thing occurred, and it was that this same day many of them fell ill. And the following day eight men died. Throughout the entire land[3] where this was known there was so much fear of us that it seemed that in seeing us

1. In this area of southwestern Texas, women once again served as intermediaries, just as Cabeza de Vaca said the women of gulf coastal areas had done (f42r).

2. Cabeza de Vaca's action apparently threatened these people, because, since traveling north from Coahuila, they had carried large bands of people with them, and each man seems to have customarily stayed with his own band or retinue in the encampments that the Indians set up for them (f50r).

3. The high plateau area of southwest Texas.

they would die of fear. They begged us not to be angry nor to will that any more of them die. And they held it for certain that we were killing them by simply desiring it. And in truth this produced in us so much anxiety that it could not have been greater, because beyond seeing those who died, we feared that all of them would die or that they would abandon us out of fear, and that all the other peoples from there onward would do the same, seeing what had happened to these people. We beseeched God our Lord to remedy it. And thus all those who had been sick began to regain their health. And we saw a thing that was of great wonder, that is, the parents and brothers and sisters and wives of those who died, upon seeing them in that state, suffered much grief, and after they died, they expressed no sentiment, neither did we see them weep nor speak to one another nor make any other gesture; neither did they dare to go to them until we ordered them to bury them. And for more than fifteen days while we were with them, we saw no one speak to anyone else nor did we see them laugh nor any small child cry, rather, because one woman wept, they took her very far from there. And with some sharp teeth of a rat they lacerated her from her shoulders to almost the bottom of her legs. And seeing this cruelty and angered by it, I asked them why they did it. And they responded that it was in order to punish her because she had wept in front of me. All these fears that they had they put in all the others who newly came to meet us, to the end that they would give us everything they had, because they knew that we took nothing and would give it all back to them. This was the most obedient people we found throughout this land and of the best nature. And they are generally very well disposed.[1] When the ill had recovered, and we had already been there for three days, the women whom we had sent out arrived, saying that they had found very few people and that all had gone to the cows, since it was that season.[2] And we ordered the ones who had been sick to remain and those who were well to go with us, and that two days' journey from there those same two women would go with two of ours to bring out people and lead them to the road to receive us. And with this, the next morning all those who were the most hardy departed with us. And after a three-day journey we stopped. And the following day Alonso del Castillo departed with the black man Estevanico, taking as guides the two women. And the one of them who was a captive led them to a river[3] that flowed between some mountains where there was a village in which her father lived. And these were the first dwellings we saw that had the semblance and appearance of houses.[4] Castillo and Estevanico arrived here. And after having spoken with the Indians, at the end of three days Castillo came to where he had left us, and he brought along five or six of those Indians. And he told how he had found houses of people and permanent settlement, and that those people ate frijoles and squash, and that he had seen maize.[5] This was the thing that gladdened us more than anything else in the world, and for this we gave infinite thanks to our Lord. And he said that the

1. These were the people who greeted the men with a bounty of piñon nuts after the men's second crossing of the Rio Grande into southwest Texas. They had insisted that they could not take the men forward but were ultimately persuaded to do so after an epidemic befell them and they attributed the death of eight of their number to the Narváez men (f51v).

2. Bison hunting grounds to the north. It was late summer or early autumn 1535, and Oviedo (609a) notes that the bison were hunted during the summer.

3. The confluence of the Río Conchos, flowing from Chihuahua, and the Rio Grande, at Presidio, Texas, and Ojinaga, Chihuahua.

4. The "people of the cows" (f53r) occupied the first permanent settlements that the party had seen since they had left the Florida Panhandle in September 1528.

5. The frijoles and squash, and the people's familiarity with maize, meant crop cultivation and steady food sources. No maize had been found by the men since their departure from the Bay of Horses on the northeastern coast of the Gulf of Mexico (f16r).

a. for us] V: *om.*

black man would come with all the people of the houses to wait for us[a] on the road near there. And for this reason we departed, and having gone a league and a half, we came upon the black man and the people who were coming to receive us, and they gave us frijoles and many squash to eat and for carrying water and robes of bison hide and other things. And because these people and those who came with us were enemies and did not get along, we took leave of the first ones, giving them what they had given us. And we went on with the others.[1] And six leagues from there, when night was already upon us, we arrived at their houses where they made great celebrations with us. We stayed here one day, and on the next day we departed and took them with us to other permanent houses where they ate the same things the others had. And from there[2] onward, there was another new custom, that is, those who knew about our arrival did not come out to receive us on the roads like the others did, but rather we found them in their houses, and they had others made for us. And they were all seated and all had their faces turned toward the wall with their heads lowered and their hair pulled over their eyes and their possessions placed in a pile in the middle of the house. And from here[3] onward, they began to give us many robes of hide. And they did not have anything that they did not give us. They are the people with the most well formed bodies we saw and of the greatest vitality and capacity and who best understood us and responded to what we asked them. And we called them the people of the cows because the greatest number of those cows are killed near there. And upstream along that river[4] for more than fifty leagues they go killing many of them.[5] These

1. These new hosts and guides are the "people of the cows"; the former guides who depart at this point are the "people of the piñon nuts" from just north of the Rio Grande in Texas.

2. The area of permanent settlements at La Junta de los Ríos.

3. La Junta de los Ríos.

4. The Rio Grande, traveling upstream through Texas from its confluence with the Río Conchos, to the northwest toward present-day El Paso, Texas.

5. Cabeza de Vaca's earlier (f34r) observations about the extent of the bison range and people who came down through the valleys hunting them were probably based on information gained here rather than on the Texas coast. This does not discredit his claim, however, that he also saw and ate bison while near the Gulf Coast.

people go completely naked in the manner of the first ones we found. The women go covered with deerskins, as do some of the men, notably the ones who are old and who are of no use in war. It is a very populous land. We asked them why they did not sow maize. They responded to us that they did this in order not to lose what they sowed because for the last two years the rains had not come and the weather had been so dry that all of them had lost all of their maize, and that they would not dare to sow again unless it first rained a great deal. And they begged us to command the heavens to rain and to ask for it for them. And we promised them to do it thus. We also wanted to know where they had brought that maize from. And they told us that it came from where the sun set, and that it grew in all that land, but that [the maize] nearest there was in that direction. We asked them by what route we could go without difficulty and that they inform us about the road since they did not wish to go there. They told us that the road was along that river[1] upstream toward the north and that in seventeen days' journey we would not find anything to eat but a fruit[2] that grew on some trees, which they crush[3] between some rocks.[c] And even after this effort it cannot be eaten because it is coarse and dry. And such was the truth, because there they showed it to us and we could not eat it. And they told us also that while going upstream along the river we would always be passing among peoples who were their enemies and spoke their same

c. grew . . . some rocks] Z: grew on some trees, that they call Chacan, between some rocks; V: they call Chacan, and that they crush between some rocks

1. The Rio Grande.

2. Oviedo (609a) says that the Indians called this fruit *masarrones*. He also says that it grew on trees and that it was not fit to be eaten by either man or beast.

3. It is probable that the name "Chacan" is an error and that the phrase "que la machacan" (that they crush) became "que llaman Chacan" (that they call Chacan), being thus transformed by the printer into the name of the fruit.

language and who did not have anything to give us to eat, but who would receive us with very good will and give us many robes of cotton and hides and other things they had, but that it still seemed to them that by no means should we take that road. Uncertain as to what we should do and which road we should take that would be more to our purpose and advantage, we stayed with them for two days.[1] They gave us frijoles and squash to eat. The manner in which they cook them is so novel that, for being such, I wanted to put it here so that the extraordinary ingenuity and industry of humankind might be seen and known in all its diversity. They do not have pots, and in order to cook what they want to eat, they fill half a large gourd with water. And they place many rocks, of those that they can most easily ignite, into the fire, and they catch fire. And when they see that they are burning, they take them with some wooden tongs and they throw them in the gourd filled with water until they make it boil with the heat of the rocks. And when they see that the water is boiling, they put in it whatever they want to make.[a] And in all this time the only thing they do is take some rocks out and put other burning ones in, so that the water boils in order to cook whatever they want.[c]

[d]After two days had passed that we were there, we decided to go in search of the maize.[2] And we did not want to follow the road of the cows because it is toward the north, and this was for us a very great detour, because we always held it for certain that going the route of the setting

a. make] V: cook

c. want.] V: want, and in such a manner they cook it.

d.] Z: *om.* V: Chapter thirty-one: Of how we followed the maize road.

1. Their choice, as Cabeza de Vaca implies they understood it, was to go to the bison-hunting lands to the north or to follow the maize road to the west. See (f51r).

2. Here the final decision to head for the South Sea is made. Contrary to common belief, it had not been decided earlier when the men were still near the Gulf Coast not far south of the Rio Grande. At that point (f47v), their intention had been to travel only slightly inland, parallel to the coast, not overland in search of the other sea. However, it is possible that their determination had been effectively made by the time Cabeza de Vaca says they told the "people of the piñon nuts" in southwestern Texas that

they wished to go "to the place where the sun set" and "to the north" (f51r, f51v) and that they had implicitly followed this course since learning in Coahuila that copper and permanent houses were to be found in that direction (f49v).

sun we would find what we desired. And thus we followed our course and traversed the entire land until coming out at the South Sea. And the fear they put into us about the great hunger that we were to endure, which, in truth, we suffered all the seventeen days' journey about which they had told us, was not sufficient to stop us from doing this. For all the days we traveled upstream,[1] they gave us many bison robes. And we did not eat their fruit,[2] but instead our sustenance each day was no more than a handful of deer fat[3] that we were always careful to conserve for this necessity. And thus we traveled all seventeen days, and at the end of them we crossed the river[4] and walked another seventeen days in the direction of the sunset over some plains and among very great sierras that are found there.[5] And there we found people who eat nothing but some powders of grass[6] for a third of the year. And because it was that season when we walked through there, we also had to eat it until, when those days ended, we found permanent houses where there was much stored maize, and they gave us a great quantity of it, as well as of flour and squash and frijoles, and mantles of cotton.[7] And we loaded those who brought us there with everything. And with this they went home the most contented people in the world. We gave many thanks to God our Lord for having brought us there where we had found so much sustenance. Among these houses some of them were made of earth. And all the rest were made of reed[i] mats. And from here we passed through more than one hundred leagues of land,[8] and we always

i. reed] Z: sleeping

1. The Rio Grande, traveling up the Texas side.

2. *Masarrones* (Oviedo 609a).

3. Also called deer suet (Smith, *Relation* 166); the men probably carried it with them from the settlement at La Junta de los Ríos.

4. The Rio Grande, in the vicinity of El Paso, Texas, and Ciudad Juárez, Chihuahua. This was the men's third and final crossing of the Rio Grande.

5. The dunes-covered desert highlands (*medranos*) and northwest-tending ranges and basins of northern Chihuahua.

6. *polvos de paja.*

7. This area of permanent settlement was either in northwestern Chihuahua at Casas Grandes or in northeastern Sonora along the Río Bavispe.

8. Through the area known archaeologically as Sonora River Culture, characterized by the cultivation of maize, frijoles, and cotton. It extended from the upper reaches of the San Miguel, Sonora, Moctezuma, and Bavispe Rivers in the north to the Yaqui, upper Mayo, Fuerte, and Sinaloa Rivers in the south (*Historia general de Sonora* 233, 241–42).

found permanent houses and many stores of maize and frijoles. And they gave us many deer and many robes of cotton, better than those of New Spain. They also gave us many beads and some coral that is found in the South Sea [and] many very fine turquoises that they acquire from toward the north. And finally they gave here everything they had, and to Dorantes[a] emeralds[1] made into arrowheads, and with these arrows they make their *areitos* and dances. And seeming to me that they were very fine, I asked them where they had obtained them. And they said they had brought them from some very high mountains that are toward the north and they bought them in exchange for plumes and parrot feathers.[2] And they said that there were villages of many people and very large houses there. Among these people we saw the most decently clad women we had ever seen in any part of the Indies.[3] They wear some shirts of cotton that reach their knees and some half sleeves over them of folds of buckskin that touch the ground. And they rub them with certain roots that are good for cleaning, and thus they have them very well cared for; they are open in the front and close with some ties. They go about with their feet covered, wearing shoes. All these people came to us so that we might touch them and make the sign of the cross over them. And in this they were so insistent that we endured it only with great difficulty, because both the sick and the healthy wanted to be blessed. It occurred many times that of the women who went with us some gave birth. And after giving birth they brought us the infants so that we could make the sign of the cross over them and

a. Dorantes] V: me they gave five

1. Precious green stone, possibly a particularly green type of turquoise.

2. Cabeza de Vaca here provides the earliest European description of long-distance trade between northwestern Mexico, the pueblo country of present-day New Mexico, and possibly central Mexico.

3. Cabeza de Vaca implicitly contrasts the highly developed peoples of northwestern Mexico with the migratory peoples of the coastal regions of the Gulf of Mexico.

c. because they . . . from the sky.] V: *om.*

e. and] V: in peace, and

touch them.[1] They always accompanied us until they left us handed over to others. And among all these peoples, it was taken for certain that we came from the sky, because all the things that they do not have or do not know the origin of, they say come from the sky.[c2] While we went with these people, we walked the entire day without eating until night. And we ate so little that they were astonished to see it. We never felt tired and in truth we were so hardened to the task that we did not even notice it. We had a great deal of authority and influence over them. And in order to conserve this we spoke to them but few times. The black man always spoke to them and informed himself about the roads we wished to travel and the villages that there were and about other things that we wanted to know. We passed through a great number and diversity of languages. With all of them God our Lord favored us, because they always understood us and we understood them. And thus we asked and they responded by signs as if they spoke our language and we theirs, because although we knew six languages, we could not make use of them in all areas because we found more than a thousand differences. Throughout all these lands those who were at war with one another later made friends in order to come to receive us and bring us everything they had. And in this manner we left the entire land and[e3] we told them by signs, because they understood us, that in heaven there was a man whom we called God, who had created the heaven and the earth, and that we adored him and served him as Lord, and that we did whatever he

1. Oviedo (610a) notes that the mothers would put a few kernels of maize in the hands of the infants, inviting the Narváez men to take the grains from them in the belief that thus they would never suffer sickness or pain.

2. Cabeza de Vaca's explanation that "from the sky" meant "origin unknown" was deleted from the Valladolid (1555) edition. See (f46r, f56v).

3. The Valladolid (1555) edition here adds "in peace" to suggest the stabilizing and civilizing influence of the Christians over the Indians.

commanded us, and that from his hand came all good things, and if thus they were to do it, it would go very well for them. And we found such great readiness in them, that if we had had an interpreter through whom we could have understood each other perfectly, we would have left all of them Christians. This we gave them to understand as best we could. And henceforth when the sun rose, with very great shouting they opened their joined hands to the sky and afterward passed them over their entire bodies. And they did the same when the sun set. They are a people of good disposition and diligent [and] well equipped to follow any course.

a.] Z: *om.* V: Chapter thirty-two: Of how they gave us the deer hearts.

[a]In the village where they gave us the emeralds, they gave Dorantes more than six hundred open hearts of deer, of which they always have great abundance for their sustenance. And because of this, we named it the village of the hearts [Corazones],[1] and through it is the entrance to many provinces that lie toward the South Sea. And if those who should go searching for it do not pass through here, they will perish, because the coast has no maize, and they eat powders of lamb's-quarters,[2] and of grass and of fish that they take in the sea with rafts because they do not have canoes. The women cover their shameful parts with grasses and straw. They are a people timid and sad. We believe that near the coast along the route of those communities that we brought [with us], there are more than a thousand leagues of populated land. And they are well provided because they sow frijoles and maize three times a year.[3] There are three kinds of deer: those of one type are the size of young bulls of Castile.[4] Among all the people, the permanent houses are *buhíos.*[b]

b. Among all . . . are *buhíos.*] V: There are permanent houses that are called *buhíos.*

1. Cabeza de Vaca and Oviedo (610a) locate Corazones, to which Oviedo (610b) referred as a cluster of settlements ("pueblos juntos"), as being twelve leagues from the coast. Its site is likely to have been in the area of Onavas on the Río Yaqui, upstream from where its tributary stream, the Río Chico, flows into it.

2. *bledos.* Cabeza de Vaca refers to a European potherb to describe the plant consumed by these Indians. Covarrubias (221b) describes *bledos* as greens known for their capacity to soothe the stomach as a digestive and states that they were commonly cooked with oil, vinegar, and salt to make them tasty.

3. Cabeza de Vaca speculates about the lands of wealth to the north on the basis of features he would see later in southern Sonora and Sinaloa (f57r, f60r).

4. Because this sentence and the ones following it abruptly change topics, it is possible that a portion of Cabeza de Vaca's original text is missing. The Valladolid (1555) edition is roughly equivalent.

And they have poison and this is from some trees about the size of apple trees, and it is not necessary to do more than gather the fruit and smear the arrow with it. And if they do not have the fruit, they break off a branch, and with a milk they draw from it, they do the same. There are many of these trees that are so poisonous that if they crush the leaves of it and soak them in some collected water, all the deer and whatever other animals that drink from it later bloat and die.[1] We were in this village for three days,[2] and a day's journey from there was another, in which we were overtaken by so much rain that, because a river[3] rose so much, we could not cross it, and we remained there for fifteen days. During this time Castillo saw, around the neck of an Indian, a buckle[4] of a sword belt, and sewn to it a horseshoe nail. He took it from him and we asked him what that object was. And they told us that they had come from the sky. We asked him further who had brought it from there. And they responded that [it was] some men who wore beards like us, who had come from the sky and arrived at that river, and who brought horses and lances and swords, and who had lanced two of them.[5] And hiding our intention as best we could, we asked them what those men had done. And they replied to us that they had gone to the sea and that they placed their lances under the water and that they also had gone under the water, and that afterward they watched them go overland[6] until sunset.[c] We gave many thanks to God our Lord for what we heard,[7] because we were doubtful of coming upon news of Christians. And at the same time we found ourselves greatly disturbed and

c. until sunset] V: toward the setting sun

1. Oviedo (618b) evidently learned in his conversations with Cabeza de Vaca in Spain in 1547 that Cabeza de Vaca had not actually seen these trees but had only heard of them.

2. Corazones or another village first mentioned in the possibly missing text (see f56r). A day's journey from there to the place where they were detained probably took them to the portion of the Río Yaqui that customarily swelled with floods, the area of today's Presa Álvaro Obregón.

3. The Río Yaqui as it begins its westerly course toward the sea, near present-day Cumuripa, where its flooding is contained today by the Presa Álvaro Obregón.

4. *hevilleta*, or *hevilla pequeña*. The iron prong that fastens the belt (Covarrubias 685a).

5. The slaving expeditions into northwestern Mexico began with Nuño de Guzmán's 1530–31 conquest of the area. The Indians' reactions and Cabeza de Vaca's concern at this moment in late 1535 or early 1536 suggest much more recent Spanish activity in the area (f57r) than Diego de Guzmán's expedition of 1533.

6. *por cima*. Cabeza de Vaca communicates the natives' observation that the horsemen submerged themselves in the water, then reemerged and departed as the natives watched their course of travel on land.

7. Oviedo (611a) reveals that when the four men encountered the Indian who wore the buckle, they had already come across other signs indicating that Christians were in the area.

saddened, believing that those men would not be but those who had come by sea to explore. But in the end, since we had such certain news of them, we made greater haste in our journey, and we always found more signs of Christians. And we said to the Indians that we were going to look for them to tell them that they should not kill them or take them as slaves,[1] nor should they take them out of their lands, nor should they do them any other harm whatsoever; and with this they were greatly pleased. We traveled through much land and we found all of it deserted, because the inhabitants of it went fleeing through the sierras without daring to keep houses or work the land for fear of the Christians. It was a thing that gave us great sorrow, seeing the land very fertile and very beautiful and very full of waterways and rivers,[2] and seeing the places deserted and burned and the people so emaciated and sick, all of them having fled and in hiding.[3] And since they did not sow, with so much hunger they maintained themselves on the bark of trees and roots. This hunger affected us in part along this entire road, because only poorly could they provide for us, being so displaced from their natural homeland[d] that it seemed that they wished to die. They brought to us beads and[e] robes that they had hidden on account of the Christians, and they gave them to us. And they even told us how other times the Christians had entered the land[4] and had destroyed and burned the villages and carried off half the men and all the women and boys, and that those who had been able to escape out of their hands now went fleeing, as we saw them so terrorized that they dared not stop in any place, and they neither wanted nor were able to

d. displaced from their natural homeland] V: wretched, miserable

e. beads and] V: *om.*

1. Cabeza de Vaca here anticipates knowledge that he could only have gained later, namely, that these were not maritime explorers but rather conquistadors in search of Indians to take as slaves.

2. The four survivors were traveling south of the Río Yaqui some ten to twelve leagues (approximately thirty to thirty-six miles or forty-eight to fifty-eight kilometers) inland from the coast, according to Oviedo (611a). These were alluvial plains of the fertile river valleys of Sonora.

3. The Indians fleeing this area went up into the ranges and low basins that rose from the plain to the escarpment of the Sierra Madre Occidental (Sauer, "The Road" map facing 58).

4. Oviedo (611b) cites three previous *entradas* or incursions into this area.

sow or work the land; rather, they were determined to let themselves die, and they considered this better than waiting to be treated with as much cruelty as they had been up to that point. And they showed very great pleasure with us, although we feared that when we arrived at the ones who held the frontier against the Christians and were at war with them, they would treat us cruelly and make us pay for what the Christians were doing to them. But since God our Lord was served to bring us to them, they began to fear and respect us as the previous ones had done, and even somewhat more, about which we were not a little amazed, by which it is clearly seen that all these peoples, to be drawn to become Christians and to obedience to the Imperial Majesty, must be given good treatment, and that this is the path most certain and no other. These people took us to a village that is in the cleft of a mountain.[1] And it is necessary to climb very rugged terrain in order to reach it. And here we found many people who were gathered together, having taken refuge out of fear of the Christians. They received us very well and gave us everything they had, and they gave us more than two thousand loads of maize that we gave to those wretched and starving ones who had brought us there. And the next day we sent out from there four messengers through the land, as we were accustomed to doing,[2] so that they might call and bring together all the people they could, to a village that is a three-day journey from there. And this done, the next day we departed with all the people who were there.[3] And we always found traces and signs of where Christians had slept. And at midday we reached our messengers who told us that they had not

1. Oviedo (611b, 613a) calculated this highland refuge to be five leagues from where the Narváez party would meet Diego de Alcaraz and his men on the Río Sinaloa and forty leagues from the Spanish settlement at Culiacán. Sauer ("The Road" 19) suggests that this might be in the sierras on one of the headwaters of the Río Sinaloa.

2. Oviedo (607a) reports that along their entire course the four survivors sent out messengers in the name of each one of them to direct new people to prepare dwellings and gather food and provisions for them.

3. At the mountain refuge in Sinaloa.

found people, because all of them went hidden through the mountains, fleeing to avoid being killed or made slaves by the Christians, and that the previous night while they were behind some trees watching what they were doing, they had seen the Christians and saw how they were bringing many Indians in chains. And those who came with us were very disturbed by this. And some of them returned to give notice through the land that Christians were coming, and these people would have done much more[b] if we had not told them not to do it and not to have fear.[1] And with this they were reassured and very pleased. Indians from a hundred leagues from there[2] were traveling with us at that time. And we could not convince them to return to their homes. And to reassure them, we slept there that night. And the next day we traveled and slept along the road. And the following day those whom we had sent out as messengers guided us to where they had seen the Christians. And arriving at the hour of vespers, we saw clearly that they had told the truth. And we understood the people to be horsemen because of the stakes to which the horses had been tied. From here, which is called the Río de Petután,[3] to the river to which Diego de Guzmán arrived,[4] to the one where we learned about the Christians,[5] there may be eighty leagues. And from there to the village where the rains had overtaken us, twelve leagues, and from there to the settlement of Corazones there were five leagues,[d] and from there to the South Sea there were twelve leagues.[6] Throughout all this land where there are mountains, we saw great evidence of gold and antimony,[7] iron, copper, and other metals.[8] Through the area where there are permanent houses it is hot, so much so that in January there is great heat. From there southward,[9] the land is uninhabited to the North Sea; it is very

b. these people would have done much more] V: many more would have done this

d. and from there to the village of Corazones there were five leagues] V: *om.*

1. Oviedo (611b–12a) gives the same account of the Indians' discovery of a deserted Spanish camp three days from the mountain village.

2. Inhabitants of the settlements of the Corazones area in Sonora, along the north-south course of the Río Yaqui probably in the area of Onavas, according to the calculations Cabeza de Vaca gives below. Oviedo (612a) says that Indians from eighty leagues back were accompanying them.

3. Also Petachán (f61v); the Petatlán, today's Río Sinaloa.

4. Río Yaqui, at some point on its east-west course, probably no more than forty miles (sixty-five kilometers) from the coast. Diego de Guzmán arrived here in 1533.

5. Either the Río Yaqui, near the base of its north-south course, or a river that Cabeza de Vaca had not previously mentioned.

6. This calculation of distance, going from south to north (from the Río Petatlán to the Río Yaqui, then to the Indian settlement of Corazones), is concluded by an east-west calculation—the distance from Corazones to the sea—of some twelve leagues (approximately

thirty-six miles or fifty-eight kilometers).

7. See (f49r).

8. Cabeza de Vaca's previous comments about the absence or presence of mountains (f16r, f35r, f47r–v) are here revealed to pertain to the promise of mineral wealth. Oviedo (618b) challenged this explicit attribution by Cabeza de Vaca of such wealth to this area from Corazones south to the Río Petatlán. See also (f60r).

9. *hazia el mediodía de la tierra.*

wretched and poor, where we suffered great and unbelievable hunger. And those who inhabit and roam that land are a people brutish and of very bad tendencies[1] and customs. The Indians who have permanent houses and those farther back pay no attention to gold and silver nor do they find that there can be any benefit from it.

d.] Z: *om.* V: Chapter thirty-three: How we came upon the track of Christians.

[d]After we saw clear signs of Christians and we understood that we were very near them, we gave many thanks to God our Lord for wanting to take us out of so sad and wretched a captivity. And may the pleasure we felt on this account be judged by every man when he considers the time we spent in that land and the dangers and hardships we endured. That night I entreated one of my companions to go after the Christians who were going through the area where we were leaving the land secured. And it was a three-day journey.[2] This they judged a troublesome undertaking, excusing themselves because of fatigue and hardship and in spite of the fact that each one of them would be able to do it better than I, on account of being hardier and younger. But seeing their will, the next day in the morning I took with me the black man and eleven Indians, and following the trail of the Christians that I found, I passed through three places where they had slept. And this day I went ten leagues. And the next morning I reached four Christians on horseback who experienced great shock upon seeing me so strangely dressed and in the company of Indians. They remained looking at me a long time, so astonished that they neither spoke to me nor managed to ask me anything. I told them to take me to their

1. *mala inclinación.*

2. Cabeza de Vaca here antici-pates information that he acquired on his search for the Christians.

captain. And thus we went half a league from there, where their captain, Diego de Alcaraz, was.[1] And after I had spoken to him, he said that he was very lost there because it had been many days since he had been able to take any Indians[2] and that there was no way to go because among them there began to be great need and hunger. I told him how Dorantes and Castillo remained behind at a place ten leagues from there with many people who had brought us. And he then sent out three horsemen and fifty Indians of those they were bringing. And the black man returned with them to guide them. And I remained there and I asked that they certify for me the year and the month and day that I had arrived there, and the manner in which I had come, and thus they did it.[3] From this river[4] to the village of the Christians, which is called San Miguel, which is under the governance of the province they call Nueva Galicia, there are thirty leagues.

[b]Five days later, Andrés Dorantes and Alonso del Castillo arrived with those who had gone for them.[5] And they brought with them more than six hundred people[6] who were from that settlement that the Christians[7] had caused to ascend into the highlands, and they went about hidden throughout the land. And those who had come with us to that point[8] had taken them out of the mountains and turned them over to the Christians,[9] and they had sent away all the other peoples whom they had brought there. And when they had arrived to where I was, Alcaraz beseeched me to call the people of the villages that are found on the bank along the river,[10] who went hidden through the mountains of the land, and command them to bring food to eat, although this was not necessary because they always took care to bring us all they could. And

b.] Z: *om.* V: Chapter thirty-four: Of how I sent for the Christians.

1. At the Río Petatlán. Alcaraz was a participant in Nuño de Guzmán's 1530–31 conquest of northwestern Mexico (Nueva Galicia) and would later serve as a captain in the Coronado expedition of 1540–42.

2. As guides and slaves; Oviedo (612a) specifies that it had been fifteen days since they had even seen an Indian.

3. In the spring of 1536, possibly April.

4. The Río Petatlán.

5. Estevanico and the men sent by Diego de Alcaraz.

6. The Indians the four men had encountered in the mountain refuge (f57v), somewhere south of their crossing of the Río Yaqui, in Sinaloa. Cabeza de Vaca and his companions had left that settlement approximately ten days earlier.

7. Alcaraz and his men.

8. Indians from the Corazones area on the north-south-running Río Yaqui in Sonora who were traveling with the men (f58r) and the ones from farther south, in Sinaloa, who held the frontier against the Spaniards and had taken the four men to the mountain retreat (f57v).

9. Dorantes and Castillo.

10. The Río Petatlán.

we then sent out our messengers to call them, and six hundred people came who brought us all the maize they could obtain. And they brought it in some clay-sealed pots in which they had buried and hidden it.[1] And they brought us everything else they had, but we refused to take any of it except the food. And we gave everything else to the Christians[2] so that they could distribute it among themselves. And after this we suffered many annoyances[b] and great disputes with them, because they wanted to enslave the Indians we brought with us. And with this anger, on parting we left many Turkish bows[3] that we carried, and many leather pouches and arrows and among them the five made from emeralds[4] that we inadvertently left, and thus we lost them. We gave the Christians many bison robes and other things that we carried. We had great difficulty convincing the Indians to return to their homes and secure themselves and sow their maize. They did not want but to go with us until leaving us with other Indians, as they were accustomed to doing, because if they returned without doing this, they feared they would die, and going with us, they feared neither the Christians nor their lances. The Christians were disturbed by this, and they made their interpreter tell them that we were of the same people as they, and that we had been lost for a long time, and that we were people of ill fortune and no worth, and that they were the lords of the[d] land whom the Indians were to serve and obey. But of all this the Indians were only superficially or not at all convinced of what they told them. Rather, some talked with others among themselves, saying that the Christians

b. annoyances] V: *om.*

d. the] V: that

1. These carefully conserved stores of maize, also described by Oviedo (612b), reveal that the Indians of southern Sonora and northern Sinaloa had been taking measures for some time to protect themselves from the slave-hunting expeditions.

2. The armed and mounted men led by Diego de Alcaraz.

3. Native weapons commonly mentioned in conquistadors' accounts of northern New Spain and Spanish Nuevo México.

4. See (f55r).

were lying, because we came from where the sun rose, and they from where it set; and that we cured the sick, and that they killed those who were well; and that we came naked and barefoot, and they went about dressed and on horses and with lances; and that we did not covet anything but rather, everything they gave us we later returned and remained with nothing, and that the others had no other objective but to steal everything they found and did not give anything to anyone. And in this manner, they conveyed everything about us and held it in high esteem to the detriment of the others. And thus they responded to the Christians' interpreter and they made known the same thing to the others through a language that they had among them by which we understood one another. And those who speak it we call Primahaitu,[1] which we found used in more than four hundred leagues of those we had traveled, and we found no other in all that distance.[e] Finally, it was not possible to convince the Indians that we were the same as the other Christians, and with much effort and insistence we made them return to their homes, and we ordered them to secure themselves and settle their villages, and to sow and work the land since, because of being abandoned, it was now very overgrown with vegetation,[2] for that land is without doubt the best of any to be found in these Indies and the most fertile and abundant in foodstuffs. And they sow three times a year.[3] They have many fruits and many beautiful rivers and many other very good waterways. There are great indications and signs of mines of gold and silver.[4] The people are of very good inclinations. Those who are friends of the Christians serve them very willingly. They are very well disposed, much more so

e. call Primahaitu . . . all that distance.] V: properly called Primahaitu (which is like saying Basques), which we found used among them in more than four hundred leagues of those we had traveled, without finding any other in all those lands.

1. A native lingua franca or trade language that no doubt facilitated the friendly reception and rapid travel of the Cabeza de Vaca party across northern Mexico.

2. *llena de monte*. The thorny scrub vegetation of cacti, small trees, and wild shrubs had overrun the alluvial plains in the five years since the Spanish had begun making incursions into the area.

3. These alluvial flood plains were nourished by early spring floods as well as summer rains, thus making possible multiple annual crop cycles.

4. Again Cabeza de Vaca suggests the possibility of mineral wealth, this time for the region of the Río Petatlán southward. See (f58r). These brief remarks helped stimulate further exploration and served as an emblem of northern riches during the subsequent two centuries.

a. And after . . . conduct,] V: After we had sent the Indians away in peace, and expressing to them our gratitude for the efforts they had made on our behalf, the Christians sent us off under the guard of an *alcalde* named Cebreros, and two others with him, who led us through overgrown and deserted areas in order to remove us from conversation with the Indians, and so that we would neither see nor learn about what they [the Christians], in fact, did, from which it is evident how much men's thoughts deceive them, for we went to them seeking liberty and when we thought we had it, it turned out to be so much to the contrary,

d.] Z: *om.* V: Chapter thirty-five: Of how the *alcalde mayor* received us well the night we arrived.

e. Upon learning] V: Since the *alcalde mayor* was advised

than those of Mexico. And, finally, it is a land that lacks nothing in order to be very good. When we dispatched the Indians, they told us that they would do what we commanded and would settle their villages if the Christians would let them. And thus I declare and affirm as true that if they should not do it, the Christians will be to blame. And after we had sent them away the Christians sent us off under the guard of an *alcalde* who was named Cebreros[1] and three other Christians with him, from which it is evident how much men's thoughts deceive them, for we went to them seeking liberty and when we thought we had it, it turned out to be so much to the contrary. And in order to remove us from conversation with the Indians, they led us through areas depopulated and overgrown so that we would not see what they were doing nor their conduct,[a] because they had conspired to go and attack the Indians whom we had sent away reassured and in peace. And they carried it out just as they had planned it.[2] They led us through those dense thickets for two days without water, lost and without a path. And we all thought that we would perish from thirst, and seven men died from it, and many friends[3] that the Christians brought with them were unable, until noon of the following day, to reach the place where we found water that night. And we walked with them twenty-five leagues, a little more or less. And at the end of them, we arrived at a village of peaceful Indians. And the *alcalde*[4] who was leading us left us there, and he went on ahead another three leagues to a settlement called Culiacán where Melchior Díaz, *alcalde mayor*[5] and captain of that province, was. [d]Upon learning[e] of our escape and arrival, he

1. Lázaro de Cebreros, who had participated in Guzmán's conquest of northwestern Mexico. In the colonial administration of Nueva Galicia in these early years the *alcalde* (first-instance judge) not only acted as a judicial officer but also presided over municipal governance (Parry, *The Audiencia* 5, 33).

2. Oviedo (613a) also reports that the Spanish slavers returned to their habitual pursuit.

3. Indians traveling with the Spanish soldiers and the Narváez survivors.

4. Lázaro de Cebreros.

5. As chief justice and civil official of the province (*alcalde mayor*), Díaz was the *alcalde* Cebreros's superior.

departed later that night and came to where we were,[1] and he wept a great deal with us, praising God our Lord for having shown so much mercy to us. And he spoke to us and treated us very well. And on behalf of the governor, Nuño de Guzmán,[2] as well as his own, he offered us everything that he had and could. And he [Melchior Díaz] showed much sorrow at the bad reception and treatment we had received from Alcaraz and the others we had found. And we took it for certain that if he had been there,[3] what was done to us and the Indians would have been prevented. And after that night, the next day we departed for Auhacán[c4] and the *alcalde mayor*[5] beseeched us earnestly to stop there; that in doing so we would perform a very great service to God our Lord[d] and Your Majesty, because the land was abandoned and not cultivated and all of it greatly destroyed, and the Indians went about hidden and in flight through the highlands without wanting to come and settle themselves in their villages; and [he asked] that we have them called together and order them on behalf of God and Your Majesty to come and settle the plain and work the land. To us this seemed very difficult to put into effect, because we did not bring any Indian of ours or any of those who usually accompanied us and were skilled in these matters. Finally we entrusted this to two Indians of those whom they held captive there, who were of that land, and these Indians had been with the Christians when we first arrived to them, and they saw the people who accompanied us[6] and learned from them about the great authority and influence that

c. for Auhacán,] V: *om.*

d. our Lord] V: *om.*

1. Three leagues from the native settlement of Culiacán and five leagues from the Spanish *villa* of San Miguel, according to Cabeza de Vaca; Oviedo (613a) said the men were eight leagues from the Spanish municipality, which he called simply the "villa de Culiacán."

2. Named governor of the province of Pánuco in 1525 and president of the First Audiencia of New Spain in 1528, Guzmán conquered northwestern Mexico in 1530–31 and was appointed governor of this new province, called Nueva Galicia, in 1531.

3. Melchior Díaz, at the Río Petatlán, or Sinaloa, when the Narváez survivors met with Alcaraz.

4. The native settlement of Culiacán, three leagues distant and two leagues from the Spanish municipality of San Miguel de Culiacán.

5. Melchior Díaz.

6. The eleven Indians from the area of Corazones and farther south in Sonora, who had accompanied Cabeza de Vaca and Estevanico (f58v), and the six hundred Indians from the mountain refuge in Sinaloa, brought by Dorantes and Castillo (f59r). The two Indian captives of Diego de Alcaraz were from the Culiacán area in Sinaloa.

through all those lands we had possessed and exercised, and the wonders that we had worked and the sick people we had cured and many other things. And with these [two] Indians we commanded other Indians of the settlement[1] to together go and call the Indians who had taken refuge in the sierras[2] and those of the Río Petachán,[a] where we had found the Christians,[3] and tell them to come to us because we desired to speak to them. And so that they could go in safety and the others come forth, we gave them a very large gourd of those that we carried in our hands, which was our principal insignia and emblem of our great estate.[4] And taking this gourd they set out and went through the area for seven days, and at the end of them, they returned and brought with them three lords, of those who were taking refuge in the sierras, who brought along fifteen men. And they brought us beads and turquoises and plumes. And the messengers told us that they had not found the natives of the river[5] where we had come out because the Christians had again made them flee to the highlands. And Melchior Díaz told the interpreter to speak on our behalf to those Indians and tell them how we came on behalf of God who is in heaven, and how we had walked through the world for nine[b] years,[6] telling all the people we had found to believe in God and serve him because he was Lord of all things in the world, and that he blessed and rewarded the good, and punished the bad with perpetual fire, and that when the good died, he carried them to heaven where no one would die or be hungry or cold or thirsty or have any other need whatsoever, but rather, would have the greatest glory that one could imagine, and that those who did not

a. Petachán] V: Petaan

b. nine] V: many

1. The native settlement of Culiacán.

2. From Culiacán north to the Río Sinaloa and beyond. Because Oviedo (613b) alone mentions native insurgency in this northernmost area of Spanish activity, he may be conflating the men's account of affairs in Sinaloa and northward with those of the region farther south, from San Miguel to Compostela (southern Sinaloa, Nayarit, and Jalisco).

3. Diego de Alcaraz and his men.

4. The men had begun to make use of the gourds in Tamaulipas (f46r, f48v).

5. The Río Petatlán (Sinaloa) and its formerly densely populated flood plain.

6. It was late April 1536; the Narváez expedition had sailed from Spain in June 1527.

want to believe in him or obey his commandments would be cast by him under the ground in the company of demons and into a great fire that would never cease, but rather torment them forever, and that beyond this, if they desired to be Christians and serve God our Lord[a] in the manner in which we commanded them, that the Christians would take them as brothers and treat them very well, and we would order them [the Christians] not to provoke them or take them out of their lands, but rather to be their great friends, but that if they did not want to do this, the Christians would treat them very badly and carry them off as slaves to other lands.[1] To this they responded to the interpreter that they would be very good Christians and serve God. And when asked to what they gave reverence and made sacrifices and whom they asked for water for their maize fields and health for themselves, they responded that it was to a man who was in the sky. We asked them what his name was. And they said it was Aguar, and that they believed that he had created the whole world and all the things in it. We again asked them how they knew this. And they responded that their fathers and grandfathers had told it to them, that for a long time they had known about this, and they knew that that man sent water and all good things. We told them that the one to whom they referred we called God, and that thus they should call him and serve and adore him as we commanded and they would be well served by it. They responded that they understood everything very well and that thus they would do it. And we ordered them to come down from the sierras and to come forward confidently and in peace, and populate the land and put up their houses and in the midst of them make one

a. our Lord] V: *om.*

1. This speech, which gave the Indians the choice between accepting Castilian rule or submitting to war and destruction, is the *requerimiento*, of which the reading on all conquest expeditions was mandated by law in November 1526.

for God and put a cross at the entrance, like the one we had there, and that when Christians came there, to come out and receive them with the crosses in their hands, without their bows and without weapons, and take them to their houses and give them whatever they had to eat, and in this way they [the Christians] would not do them harm but rather would be their friends. And they said that thus they would do it as we commanded it. And the captain[1] gave them robes and treated them very well, and thus they returned, taking the two who were captives and who had gone as messengers. This occurred in the presence of the notary they had there and many other witnesses.[2]

a.] Z: *om*. V: Chapter thirty-six: Of how we had churches built in that land.

[a]When the Indians returned,[3] all those of that province[4] who were friends[5] of the Christians, since they had news of us, came to see us. And they brought us beads and plumes. And we commanded them to build churches and put crosses in them, because until then they had not made them. And we had them bring the children of the most important lords and baptize them.[6] And afterward, the captain made a solemn oath to God to neither make nor consent to making any incursion nor to take slaves in that land or among people whom we had secured, and that this he would uphold and fulfill until His Majesty and the governor Nuño de Guzmán or the viceroy[7] in his name acted to comply with what would best serve God our Lord[c] and His Majesty. And after the children had been baptized, we departed for the *villa* of San Miguel,[8] where, when we arrived, Indians came who told us how many people were coming down from the sierras and populating the plain and making churches and crosses and doing everything we had commanded them. And each

c. our Lord] V: *om*.

1. Melchior Díaz.

2. The notary and witnesses legally certified the pact made with the natives. This occurred at the native settlement of Culiacán (f61v).

3. The three native lords and fifteen other Indians from the sierras where they had taken refuge and whom the two captive Indians of Culiacán had brought down on the order of Melchior Díaz (f61r–v).

4. Culiacán.

5. Allies or slaves of the Spaniards settled at Culiacán.

6. *hijos*. Probably only male children; the baptism of the sons of native lords was a common religious intervention in the earliest peaceful contacts between Europeans and Indians in the Indies.

7. Antonio de Mendoza, first viceroy of New Spain (1535–50).

8. Mentioned earlier (f59r), San Miguel was located two leagues (eight leagues; Oviedo 613a) beyond the native settlement of Culiacán, where Cabeza de Vaca and his companions had resettled the natives of the region at Melchior Díaz's request (f61v–f62v).

day we received news of how this was being most fully carried out and accomplished.[1] And after we had been there fifteen days,[2] Alcaraz arrived with the Christians who had gone on that raid. And they told the captain[3] how the Indians were down from the sierras and had populated the plain, and they had found populous villages that earlier were abandoned and deserted, and that the Indians came out to receive them with crosses in their hands and took them to their houses and shared with them what they had. And they slept with them there that night. Astonished by such a new development and by what the Indians told them about how they were now secured, he ordered that they do them no harm and thus they took leave.

May God our Lord in his infinite mercy grant, in all the days of Your Majesty and under your authority and dominion, that these people come and be truly and with complete devotion subject to the true Lord who created and redeemed them. And we hold it for certain that it will be so, and that Your Majesty will be the one who is to put this into effect, that it will not be so difficult to do, because in the two thousand leagues[4] that we traveled by land and through the sea on the rafts and another ten months[5] that we went through the land[6] without stopping once we were no longer captives, we found neither sacrifices nor idolatry. In this period we crossed from one sea to the other,[7] and by the information that with very great effort we acquired, [we came] to understand [that] from one coast to the other at its widest point, the distance may be two hundred leagues.[8] And we came to know that on the coast of the South [Sea] there are pearls and many

1. Oviedo (613a) ends here his account of the four men's journey.

2. At the *villa* of San Miguel de Culiacán, for two weeks (1 May–15 May) in 1536.

3. Melchior Díaz.

4. This estimate of the distance traveled comprehends the entire course of the men's journey from the Florida Cape to San Miguel de Culiacán in Sinaloa.

5. Roughly from midsummer 1535 to May 1536.

6. From the coastal areas of southeastern Texas through Tamaulipas, Nuevo León, and Coahuila into southwestern Texas along the Rio Grande, through Chihuahua, Sonora, and Sinaloa to San Miguel de Culiacán.

7. From the North Sea (Gulf of Mexico) to the South Sea (Gulf of California).

8. Some 600 miles (approximately 990 kilometers), a considerable underestimation of the breadth of North America at the latitudes at which the four Narváez survivors crossed it.

riches and that all the best and richest things are near it.

We were in the *villa* of San Miguel until the fifteenth of May, and the reason for stopping there so long was that from there to the city of Compostela[1] where the governor Nuño de Guzmán resided, the distance is one hundred leagues, and all are deserted and in enemy hands.[2] And it was necessary that we travel in the company of others among whom were twenty horsemen who accompanied us as far as forty leagues.[3] And from there onward six Christians, who brought with them five hundred Indian slaves, came with us. And having arrived in Compostela, the governor received us very well and from the provisions he had gave us some clothes, which I was unable to wear for many days, nor were we able to sleep but on the ground. And after ten or twelve days had passed, we left for Mexico.[4] And along the entire road we were well treated by the Christians. And many came out to see us along the roads and gave thanks to God our Lord[b] for having delivered us from so many dangers. We arrived in [the city of] Mexico on Sunday, one day before the eve of Saint James, where we were very well treated and received with much pleasure by the viceroy[5] and the marqués del Valle.[6] And they gave us clothes to wear and offered everything they had, and on the day of Saint James[7] there were fiestas and *juegos de cañas*[8] and bullfights.

[c]After we rested in Mexico for two months,[9] I attempted to come to these kingdoms.[10] And going to embark[11] in the month of October, there came a storm that capsized the ship and it was lost. And having seen this, I decided to let the winter pass, because in those parts it is a very harsh season in which to navigate.[12]

b. our Lord] V: *om.*

c.] Z: *om.* V: Chapter thirty-seven: Of what occurred when I attempted to come [here, i.e., to Castile].

---

1. In 1536, the capital of Nueva Galicia, located in present-day Jalisco.

2. The Indians of southern Sinaloa, Nayarit, and Jalisco had abandoned their agricultural communities and were making war on the Spanish invaders.

3. *hasta quarenta leguas.* The Spanish cavalry accompanied the men either forty leagues from San Miguel or to within forty leagues of Compostela.

4. México-Tenochtitlán, capital of New Spain and former seat of the Aztec confederation, which fell to Hernán Cortés in 1521.

5. Antonio de Mendoza.

6. Hernán Cortés, titled by the emperor in 1528.

7. 25 July; the Sunday before was 23 July 1536.

8. Jousts in which teams of horsemen, riding at full speed, hurled wooden lances called *cañas* at one another.

9. Approximately August and September 1536, during which time the three Castilians prepared the Joint Report for the emperor and the Audiencia of Santo Domingo.

10. The kingdoms of Spain: Castile, Aragon, and Navarre.

11. From Veracruz.

12. See (f3v–f5v) on the severity of the winter weather in the Caribbean.

b. another] V: others

And after the winter had passed, during Lent[1] Andrés Dorantes and I departed from [the city of] Mexico for Veracruz to embark. And we were there waiting for a wind until Palm Sunday when we embarked, and we waited aboard more than fifteen days for lack of wind. And the ship we were in took on much water. I left the ship and went to another[b] of those that were about to leave, and Dorantes remained in that one.[2] And on the tenth of April we departed from the port in three ships and we sailed together one hundred and fifty leagues. And en route two of the ships took on much water, and one night we lost their company, because the pilots and helmsmen, according to what we later found out, did not dare to go on ahead with their ships and returned back to the port from which they had departed without our realizing it or being informed about them. And we continued our journey. And on the fourth of May we arrived at the port of Havana, which is on the island of Cuba, where we were waiting for the other two ships,[3] believing that they would come, until the second day of June when we departed from there with much fear of encountering French ships, since it had been only a few days since they had taken three of our ships there. And arriving in the vicinity of the island of Bermuda, we were caught in a storm that usually overtakes all those who pass through there, which agrees with what the people who frequent that island say, and for one entire night we believed we were doomed. But it pleased God that, come the morning, the storm ceased and we followed our course. And at the end of twenty-nine days since we had departed from Havana, we had gone one thousand and one hundred leagues, which they say is the distance from there to the outpost at the Azores,

1. Spring 1537.

2. They were to travel in a three-ship convoy loaded with gold and silver (f64r, f65r).

3. The arrival of Cabeza de Vaca's ship at Havana, loaded with gold and silver and having lost the other two members of its convoy, is recorded in a 31 May 1537 letter from Juan Velázquez to the Casa de la Contratación (CDU 6:22–23).

and continuing the following day to the island that they call Corvo, we confronted a French ship.[1] At the hour of midday, it began to follow us with a Portuguese caravel[2] it had taken. And they pursued us.[3] And that afternoon we saw another nine sails, and they were so far away that we could not determine if they were Portuguese or of those same ones that were following us. And when night fell the French ship was the distance of a cannon shot from our ship, and as soon as it was dark, we changed our course in order to get away from it. And since it was sailing so close to us, it saw what we had done and cut off our path, and we did this three or four times. And it could have taken us if it wanted, but it left the task for the morning. It pleased God that, when morning came, we and the French ship found ourselves together and very near the nine ships that I said we had seen the previous afternoon, which we recognized as belonging to the Portuguese armada. And I gave thanks to God for having escaped from the hardships of the land and the perils of the sea. And the French ship, when it recognized the Portuguese armada, released the caravel that it held captive, which was coming loaded with black people, which it [the French ship] carried with it to make us believe that they were [both] Portuguese ships so that we would wait for them. And when it [the French ship] released it [the Portuguese caravel], it told the helmsman and the pilot of it that we were French and part of its convoy. And having said this, it put out sixty oars from the ship. And thus by oar and sail it set out, and it went so fast it is not to be believed. And the [Portuguese] caravel that it released went to the galleon.[4] And it told its captain that our ship and the other one were French. And when our ship approached the galleon, and since the entire

1. French pirates menaced the Spanish ship on which Cabeza de Vaca was traveling and attempted to make both the Spanish ship and the Portuguese slave ship they had already captured think that the other was foe, not friend.

2. A Portuguese slave ship, as described below (f64v).

3. The French corsair, bringing the Portuguese caravel that it had captured earlier, began to pursue the ship on which Cabeza de Vaca was traveling.

4. The commanding ship of the Portuguese armada. "Galeón"

is confusing, because Cabeza de Vaca uses it to refer to both the French corsair as well as the flagship of the Portuguese armada.

armada saw that we were coming at them, taking it for certain that we were French, they readied themselves for war and came at us. And arriving near one another, we saluted them. Recognizing that we were friends, they realized that they had been tricked into allowing that corsair to escape by having said that we were French and in their company, and thus four caravels went after it. And when the galleon arrived to us, after having saluted them, the captain, Diego de Silveira, asked us where we were coming from and what cargo we carried. And we responded that we were coming from New Spain, and that we were carrying silver and gold. And he asked us how much. The helmsman told him that we were carrying about three hundred thousand *castellanos*.[1] The captain responded [in Portuguese]: "You certainly come with great riches, but you bring a very bad ship and very bad artillery! Son of a bitch, there's that renegade French ship and what a good mouthful she's lost! Now then, since you've escaped, follow me and don't get separated from me, for with the help of God, I'll get you to Castile." And a little while later the caravels that had pursued the French ship returned because it seemed to them that it was getting away from them and because they did not want to leave the armada, which was going as escort to three ships that were coming loaded with spices.[2] And thus we arrived at the island of Terceira where we rested for fifteen days, taking on new provisions and waiting for another ship that was coming loaded from India, which was part of the convoy of the three ships that the armada was bringing. And when fifteen days had passed, we departed from there with the armada, and we arrived at the port of Lisbon on the ninth of August, the eve of Saint

1. Treasure from the Indies was expressed in *pesos*. The *castellano*, or *peso de oro*, was 450–490 *maravedís* worth of gold and silver.

2. Coming from India, this armada may have been carrying cargoes of pepper from India's Malabar coast, cinnamon from Ceylon (Sri Lanka), and the "luxury spices" of cloves, nutmeg, and mace from the islands of eastern Indonesia.

a. Llorente] V: Laurencio

Lawrence[a] in the year 1537. And because the truth is thus as I tell it above in this account, I signed it with my name.

Cabeza de Vaca.

(The account from which this was taken was signed with his name and appeared with his coat of arms.)[1]

c.] Z: *om.* V: Chapter thirty-eight: Of what happened to the rest of those who had come to the Indies.

[c]And since I have made an account of all that is mentioned above about my journey and arrival and departure from the land until returning to these kingdoms, I want as well to make a record and account of what the ships and the people who remained in them did, which I have not recorded in what I have told above because we did not have news of them until after we returned, when we found many of them in New Spain and others here in Castile, from whom we learned about the outcome and the entire end of it, in what manner it occurred.[2]

After we left the three ships (because the other one had been lost on the rugged coast),[3] which remained in grave danger, there remained in them with few provisions about one hundred persons, among whom were ten married women. And one of them had told the governor many things that happened to him on the journey before they took place. And this woman told him when he entered the land that he should not go inland because she believed that neither he nor any one of those who went with him would escape from the land, and that if one of them were to come out, God would perform great miracles through him, but that she believed that those who escaped would be few or none at all. And the governor then responded to her

1. The publisher's note, verifying the authenticity of the manuscript by attesting to the fact that it bore Cabeza de Vaca's signature and coat of arms. Although a sixteenth-century variant manuscript of Cabeza de Vaca's *Florida* account exists in the Österreichische Nationalbibliothek in Vienna (Nieto Nuño), an authenticated manuscript bearing Cabeza de Vaca's signature and coat of arms has not been discovered.

2. Cabeza de Vaca here refers back to what occurred after he departed from the ships near present-day Tampa Bay, Florida, with Narváez and his

party of three hundred men on 1 May 1528 (f8v).

3. Cabeza de Vaca states that this final entry in his *relación* includes only those things that occurred on the ships after his departure. He nevertheless adds two episodes—the loss of a ship on the Florida coast and the incident that occurred between Narváez and a woman on the expedition who spoke of the predictions of the Muslim woman (*mora*) from Hornachos—that had occurred before he and the others left on the overland expedition and that he more logically should have told near the beginning of his narrative (f8v).

that he and all those who entered with him were going to fight and conquer many and very strange peoples and lands, and that he held it for very certain that in conquering them, many would die, but those who remained would be of good fortune and would end up very rich, according to the information that he had about the wealth that there was in that land. And he said to her, that more than he entreated her to tell him the things that she had said about deeds past and present, [to tell him] who had told them to her. She replied to him and said that in Castile a Moorish woman from Hornachos[1] had told it to her (which account she had told us before we departed from Castile), and the entire voyage had occurred to us in the same manner that she had told us. And after the governor had left Caravallo, a native of Cuenca de Huete, as his lieutenant and captain of all the ships and people that he left there,[2] we departed from them, the governor leaving them instructed later and by every possible means to gather the ships together and pursue their journey, following directly along the route to the [Río] Pánuco and always going along the coast and seeking the port as best they could, and upon finding it, to stop in it and wait for us.[3] During that time that they gathered themselves into the ships, they say that those people who were there saw and heard—all of them very clearly—how that woman said to the other women that since their husbands were entering inland and were putting themselves in such great peril, they should not count in any way on them, and that they should look to see whom they might marry, because she planned so to do it.

1. Hornachos, in Badajoz, Extremadura, was well known throughout the sixteenth century for its almost exclusively Morisco population.

2. Near Tampa Bay, Florida. Narváez had left Caravallo in charge of the three remaining ships and a hundred persons (including ten women) on 1 May 1528 (f8v).

3. Caravallo had been instructed to stay close to the coast, heading north and west along the northern coast of the Gulf of Mexico in search of the Río de las Palmas and evidently also the settlement of Santisteban del Puerto on the Río Pánuco.

And thus it happened that she and the rest of the women married and lived with[1] the men who remained on the ships. And after leaving from there, the ships set sail and continued their voyage, and they found no port ahead, and they turned back. And five leagues below where we had disembarked, they found the port that entered seven or eight leagues inland, and it was the same one that we had discovered, where we found the crates from Castile that have previously been mentioned, in which were the bodies of the dead men, who were Christians.[2] And into this port and along this coast went the three ships and the other one that came from Havana and the brigantine, looking for us for nearly a year. And since they did not find us, they went on to New Spain. This port[b3] is the best in the world, and it enters inland seven or eight leagues. And it is six fathoms deep at the entrance, and five near land. And its bottom is of soft, fine sand. And there is no tide nor any fierce storm that enters it, and thus many ships will fit in it. It has a great quantity of fish. It lies one hundred leagues from Havana, which is a settlement of Christians in Cuba, and it lies in a line north to south with this town. And here breezes are always blowing. And ships come and go from one place to the other in four days, because they come and go a quarter of the crew always rowing.[4]

And since I have given an account of the ships, it is appropriate that I mention those whom our Lord was served to allow to escape from these sufferings, and the places in these kingdoms from which they come. The first is Alonso del Castillo Maldonado, a native of Salamanca, son of

b. port] V: port of which we speak

1. *amançebaron.*

2. The ships sailed north from the site where the overland contingent had set out, which was five leagues north of the mouth of Tampa Bay. Unable to find the bay and port formed by the mouth of the Río de las Palmas or the Río Pánuco that they had expected to be no more than fifteen leagues distant, they turned back, sailing south beyond the point where the overland expedition had disembarked, and continued on into Old Tampa Bay, where Narváez's exploratory land missions had found the crates containing the corpses (f7r).

3. Tampa Bay.

4. *a quartel.* Covarrubias (890b) defined *quartel* as a military term referring to the division of the corps into four companies. "Bogar a quarteles" refers to turns at rowing, by which some oarsmen row while others rest, alternating in the course of the voyage.

Doctor Castillo and of Doña Aldonza Maldonado. The second is Andrés Dorantes, son of Pablo Dorantes, a native of Béjar and a resident of Gibraleón. The third is Álvar Núñez Cabeza de Vaca, son of Francisco de Vera and grandson of Pedro de Vera, the one who conquered [Gran] Canaria, and his mother was named Doña Teresa Cabeza de Vaca, a native of Jerez de la Frontera. The fourth is named Estevanico; he is an Arabic-speaking black man, a native of Azamor.[1]

a

a.] Z: *om.* V: *Deo gracias*

b. Fine] V: *om.*

Fine[b]

The present treatise was printed in the magnificent, noble, and very ancient city of Zamora, by the honorable gentlemen Augustín de Paz and Juan Picardo, associates and printers of books, residents of the said city. At the cost and expenditure of the virtuous gentleman Juan Pedro Musetti, book merchant, resident of Medina del Campo. It was finished on the sixth day of the month of October in the year after the birth of our Savior Jesus Christ, fifteen hundred and forty-two.[c2]

c. The present treatise . . . forty-two.] V: [V:f164v] Printed in Valladolid, by Francisco Fernández de Córdoba. In the year fifteen hundred and fifty-five.

1. Azemmour, a city on the northwestern coast of Africa, located at the mouth of the Oum er Rbia River in the province of Doukkala in the kingdom of Morocco, was held by the Portuguese from 1508 (Leo Africanus 125, 126n303).

2. There are three known surviving copies of this original edition: one in the British Library, another in the John Carter Brown Library, and a third in the New York Public Library.

Appendix: 1555 Edition License to Print

1. The address of Cabeza de Vaca as governor evidently referred to his former title of governor of the province of Río de la Plata, granted by the crown in 1540 and rescinded in 1551 as a result of the sentence issued against him by the Council of the Indies because of his conduct in office. The confusing reference to Cabeza de Vaca as governor in connection with his account of Governor Narváez's *Florida* expedition is apparently the crown's conflation of Cabeza de Vaca's first voyage to the Indies as treasurer under Narváez with his second one to Río de la Plata as governor.

2. To the degree that Pero Hernández's *Commentaries*, an apology and defense of Cabeza de Vaca's governorship of the province of Río de la Plata, included "customs of the people and conditions of the land," it pertained to the band across South America from the twenty-sixth to the thirty-sixth parallel, including the area of today's southern Brazil, southern Paraguay, Uruguay, and northern Argentina.

3. The Infanta Juana (1535–73), daughter of Charles V and Isabel of Portugal and married in 1552 to João III of Portugal, acting as regent for her brother, Prince Philip.

4. From 1543 to 1556, Philip served as regent of Spain in the absence of his father, Charles V; on 16 January 1556, Charles V renounced the crown of Castile and León, together with the kingdom of Navarre and the viceroyalties of the Indies, in favor of his son (Lynch 56–57, 107–08).

5. Interim secretary in the Council of War within the Council of the Indies since 1548 (Schäfer, *El Consejo Real* 1:77, 369, 412).

The King:

Inasmuch as you, on your own behalf, Governor Álvar Núñez Cabeza de Vaca, resident of the city of Seville, have informed us that you had composed a book entitled *The Account of What Occurred in the Indies* about the expedition on which you went as governor,[1] and likewise had had another composed, entitled *Commentaries*, which treats the conditions of the land and the customs of its people.[2] The aforementioned was an effort very beneficial to the persons who were to pass through those places. And because the one book and the other were on the same subject, and it was advisable that the two should be put into one volume, you petitioned us to give you license and authorization to print and sell them for ten or twelve years, in consideration of the benefit and utility that was being derived from them, or as our judgment mandated. This matter having been examined by the members of our Council, together with the said books of which mention is made above, it was agreed that we should order that this our warrant be given in the stated case. For which we give you license and authorization, for the period of the next ten years, which shall be counted onward from the day of the date of this our warrant, that you or whoever has your power of attorney, may print and sell in these our kingdoms the said books of which mention is made above, both in one volume, the typesetting of them first being valuated by our Council, and putting this our warrant with the said valuation at the beginning of the said book, and not in any other manner. And we order that during the said time of the said ten years, no person may print or sell it without having your said power of attorney under the penalty of losing whatever printing he might have made and sold, and the body of printing type and equipment with which he made it, and in addition, of incurring a fine of ten thousand *maravedís*, which are to be apportioned, one third to the person who accused him, and another third to the judge who sentenced him, and the other third to our Council. And we order any and all of our courts of justice and each one in its jurisdiction to uphold, fulfill, and carry out this our said warrant and that which is contained in it, and that they neither deviate from, nor overlook, nor consent to the deviation from or omission of its literal content and form, and that each one who might do to the contrary be fined, under the penalty of whatever amount our judgment decrees as well as ten thousand *maravedís* for our Council. Declared in the *villa* of Valladolid on the twenty-first day of the month of March in the year fifteen hundred and fifty-five.

The Princess.[3]
By order of His Majesty,[4] Her Highness on his behalf.
Francisco de Ledesma.[5]

BIBLIOGRAPHY

Abbreviations

AGI   Archivo General de Indias

CDI   *Colección de documentos inéditos . . . de América y Oceanía*

CDU   *Colección de documentos inéditos . . . de Ultramar*

DRAE   Real Academia Española, *Diccionario de la lengua española*

Unpublished Documentary Sources

❧ Archivo General de Indias. Seville, Spain.

Casa de la Contratación 3309, 32–4-29/35, f1–f58.

    1527–88. "Libro de la Florida de capitulaciones y asiento de gobernadores y generales y adelantamientos . . . desde el año de 1527 hasta el año de 1578."

Indiferente General 421, 139–1-7.

    27 March 1528. "Carta del rey a Álvar Núñez Cabeza de Vaca."

Patronato 57, no. 4, ramo 1:f1r–f19r.

    1547. "Información hecha en el Audiencia Real de la Nueva España a pedimiento de Alonso del Castillo Maldonado de los servicios que ha hecho a Su Magestad."

Works Cited

Adorno, Rolena, and Patrick Charles Pautz. *Álvar Núñez Cabeza de Vaca: His Account, His Life, and the Expedition of Pánfilo de Narváez.* 3 vols. Lincoln: U of Nebraska P, 1999.

Alves, Abel A. "Estevan." *Historic World Leaders.* Ed. Anne Commire and Deborah Klegner. Detroit: Gale Research, 1994. 256–61.

Angelino, Henry, and Charles L. Shedd. "A Note on Berdache." *American Anthropologist* 57 (1955): 121–26.

Barcia Carballido y Zúñiga, Andrés González de, ed. "Naufragios de Álvar Núñez Cabeza de Vaca, y relación de la jornada que hizo a la Florida con el adelantado Pánfilo de Narváez." 1731. By Álvar Núñez Cabeza de

Vaca. *Historiadores primitivos de las Indias Occidentales, que juntó, traduxo en parte y sacó a luz, ilustrados con eruditas notas y copiosos índices, el ilustríssimo señor D. Andrés González Barcia, del consejo, y cámara de S[u] M[agestad]*. Vol. 1. Madrid, 1749. 43 pp. (separate pagination; "tabla" lacks foliation). 3 vols. 1749.

Baym, Nina, ed. *The Norton Anthology of American Literature*. 4th ed. New York: W. W. Norton and Company, 1994.

Bruce-Novoa, Juan. "Naufragio en los mares de la significación: De La relación de Cabeza de Vaca a la literatura chicana." *Plural* 221 (1990): 12–21.

Campbell, T. N., and T. J. Campbell. *Historic Indian Groups of the Choke Canyon Reservoir and Surrounding Area, Southern Texas*. Choke Canyon Series 1. San Antonio: Center for Archaeological Research, University of Texas at San Antonio, 1981.

Casas, Bartolomé de las. *Apologética historia sumaria*. [1555–59.] Ed. Edmundo O'Gorman. 2 vols. Serie de historiadores y cronistas de Indias 1. Mexico City: Instituto de Investigaciones Históricas, Universidad Nacional Autónoma de México, 1967.

Castile. *Las siete partidas del sabio rey, don Alonso el nono [sic], nuevamente glosadas por el licenciado Gregorio López, del Consejo Real de Indias de Su Majestad*. Laws, statutes, etc. 1555. 7 vols. Valladolid, Spain: Diego Fernández de Córdoba, 1587. 4 vols.

Chardon, Roland. "The Elusive Spanish League: A Problem of Measurement in Sixteenth-Century New Spain." *Hispanic American Historical Review* 60 (1980): 294–302.

Clayton, Lawrence A., Vernon James Knight, Jr., and Edward C. Moore, eds. *The De Soto Chronicles: The Expedition of Hernando de Soto to North America in 1539–43*. 2 vols. Tuscaloosa: U of Alabama P, 1993.

Colección de documentos inéditos relativos al descubrimiento, conquista y organización de las antiguas posesiones españolas de América y Oceanía. 42 vols. Madrid, 1864–84.

Colección de documentos inéditos relativos al descubrimiento, conquista y organización de las antiguas posesiones españolas de Ultramar. 25 vols. Madrid, 1885–1932.

Coopwood, Bethel. "The Route of Cabeza de Vaca." *Texas State Historical Association Quarterly* 3 (1899–1900): 108–40, 177–208, 229–64; 4 (1900–01): 1–32.

Cortés, Hernán. *Cartas de relación*. Ed. Ángel Delgado Gómez. Clásicos Castalia 198. Madrid: Castalia, 1993.

Covarrubias Horozco, Sebastián de. *Tesoro de la lengua castellana o española*. 1611. Ed. Martín de Riquer. Barcelona: S. A. Horta, 1943.

Covey, Cyclone, trans. *Cabeza de Vaca's Adventures in the Unknown Interior of America*. Epilogue by William T. Pilkington. By Álvar Núñez Cabeza de Vaca. New York: Collier Books, 1961.

Davenport, Harbert, and Joseph K. Wells. "The First Europeans in Texas, 1528–1536." *Southwestern Historical Quarterly* 22 (1918–19): 111–42, 205–59.

Favata, Martín A., and José B. Fernández, trans. *The Account: Álvar Núñez Cabeza de Vaca's "Relación"*. Houston: Arte Público Press, 1993.

Gates, Henry Louis, Jr., and Nellie Y. McKay, eds. *The Norton Anthology of African American Literature*. New York: W. W. Norton and Company, 1997.

Gerhard, Peter. *The North Frontier of New Spain*. Princeton, N.J.: Princeton UP, 1982.

Hemming, John. *The Conquest of the Incas*. New York: Harcourt Brace Jovanovich, 1970.

Historia general de Sonora: I. Periodo prehistórico y prehispánico. Coordinated by Sergio Calderón Valdés. Vol. 1. Hermosillo: Gobierno del Estado de Sonora, 1985. 5 vols. 1985.

Hodge, Frederick W., ed. *The Narrative of Álvar Núñez Cabeça de Vaca*. Trans. Buckingham Smith. In *Spanish Explorers in the Southern United States, 1528–1543*. New York: Charles Scribner's Sons, 1907. 1–126.

Jefferson, Thomas. *The Papers of Thomas Jefferson. Volume 11: 1 January to 6 August 1787*. Ed. Julian P. Boyd, Mina R. Bryan, and Frederick Aandahl. Princeton, N.J.: Princeton UP, 1955. 29 vols. 1955–2002.

Krieger, Alex D. "Un nuevo estudio de la ruta seguida por Cabeza de Vaca a través de Norte América." Diss. Universidad Nacional Autónoma de México, 1955.

Lafaye, Jacques. "Los 'milagros' de Álvar Núñez Cabeza de Vaca (1527–1536)." *Mesías, cruzadas, utopías: El judeo-cristianismo en las sociedades ibéricas*. Trans. Juan José Utrilla. Mexico City: Fondo de Cultura Económica, 1984. 65–84.

Lea, Henry Charles. *A History of the Inquisition of Spain*. 4 vols. New York: Macmillan, 1907. 1906–07.

Leal, Luis. "Mexican American Literature: A Historical Perspective." In *Modern Chicano Writers: A Collection of Critical Essays*. Ed. Joseph Sommers and Tomás Ybarra-Frausto. Englewood Cliffs, N.J.: Prentice-Hall, 1979. 18–30.

Leo Africanus, Joannes. *Description de l'Afrique*. Trans. and ed. Alexis Épaulard. Vol. 1. Paris: Librairie d'Amérique et d'Orient, Adrien-Maisonneuve, 1956. 2 vols. Translation of *Descrizione dell'Africa*. 1526.

Lévi-Strauss, Claude. *Structural Anthropology*. Trans. Claire Jacobson and Brooke Grundfest Schoepf. Garden City, N.Y: Doubleday, 1967. Translation of *Anthropologie Structurale*. 1958.

Lynch, John. *Spain under the Habsburgs. Volume One: Empire and Absolutism 1516–1598*. 1964. 2nd ed. New York: New York UP, 1981. 2 vols.

Mena, Juan de. *Laberinto de fortuna*. Ed. and introduction by John G. Cummins. Letras hispánicas 110. Madrid: Cátedra, 1984.

Nieto Nuño, Miguel, ed. *Historia en español de las Indias del Nuevo Mondo (Naufragios). Codex vindobonensis 5620. Österreichische Nationalbibliothek, Viena*. By Álvar Núñez Cabeza de Vaca. 2 vols. Madrid: Guillermo Blázquez, 1996.

Núñez Cabeza de Vaca, Álvar. *La relación que dio Álvar Núñez Cabeça de Vaca de lo acaescido en las Indias en la armada donde iva por governador Pánphilo de Narbáez, desde el año de veinte y siete hasta el año de treinta y seis que bolvió a Sevilla con tres de su compañía*. Zamora: Printed by Augustín de Paz and Juan Picardo for Juan Pedro Musetti, 1542.

———. *La relación y comentarios del governador Álvar Núñez Cabeça de Vaca, de lo acaescido en las dos jornadas que hizo a las Indias*. Valladolid, Spain: Francisco Fernández de Córdova, 1555.

Oviedo y Valdés, Gonzalo Fernández de. *Historia general y natural de las Indias, islas y tierra firme del mar océano*. [1525–48.] Ed. José Amador de los Ríos. 4 vols. Madrid: Real Academia de la Historia, 1851–55.

Pagden, Anthony, trans. and ed. *Letters from Mexico*. By Hernán Cortés. Introduction by J. H. Elliott. 1971. New Haven, Conn.: Yale UP, 1986.

Panger, Daniel. *Black Ulysses*. Athens: Ohio UP, 1982.

Parish, Helen Rand. *Estebanico*. New York: Viking Press, 1974.

Parry, John H. *The Audiencia of New Galicia in the Sixteenth Century: A Study in Spanish Colonial Government*. Cambridge: Cambridge UP, 1948.

Pilkington, William T. "Epilogue." In Covey, *Cabeza de Vaca's Adventures*, 145–51.

Ponton, Brownie, and Bates McFarland. "Álvar Núñez Cabeza de Vaca: A Preliminary Report on His Wanderings in Texas." *Texas State Historical Association Quarterly* 1 (1898): 166–86.

Pupo-Walker, Enrique, ed. *Los Naufragios*. By Álvar Núñez Cabeza de Vaca. Nueva biblioteca de erudición y crítica 5. Madrid: Castalia, 1992.

Radin, Paul. *The Trickster: A Study in American Indian Mythology*. 1956. Introduction by Stanley Diamond. Commentaries by Karl Kerényi and C. G. Jung. New York: Schocken Books, 1972.

Real Academia Española. *Diccionario de la lengua española*. 19th ed. Madrid: Talleres gráficos de la Editorial Espasa-Calpe, 1970.

Sauer, Carl O. "The Road to Cíbola." *Ibero-Americana* 3 (1932): 1–58.

Schäfer, Ernesto. *El Consejo Real y Supremo de las Indias*. 2 vols. Seville: Universidad de Sevilla, Escuela de Estudios Hispano-Americanos, 1935–47.

Schnarch, Brian. "Neither Man nor Woman: Berdache—A Case for Non-Dichotomous Gender Construction." *Anthropologica* 34 (1992): 105–21.

Serrano y Sanz, Manuel, ed. *Relación de los naufragios y comentarios de Álvar Núñez Cabeza de Vaca*. 2 vols. Colección de libros y documentos referentes a la historia de América 5, 6. Madrid: Victoriano Suárez, 1906.

Sheridan, Guillermo. *Cabeza de Vaca: inspirada libremente en el libro Naufragios, de Álvar Núñez Cabeza de Vaca*. Prologue by Álvaro Mutis, introduction by Nicolás Echevarría. Mexico City: El Milagro, 1994.

Simon and Schuster's International Dictionary: English/Spanish, Spanish/English. General editor, Tana de Gámez. New York: Simon and Schuster, 1973.

Smith, Buckingham, trans. *The Narrative of Álvar Núñez Cabeça de Vaca*. Washington, D.C., 1851.

———. *Relation of Álvar Núñez Cabeça de Vaca*. New York, 1871. Rpt. March of America Facsimile Series 9. Ann Arbor, Mich.: University Microfilms, 1966.

Vas Mingo, Milagros del. *Las capitulaciones de Indias en el siglo XVI*. Madrid: Instituto de Cooperación Iberoamericana, 1986.

Vedia, Enrique de, ed. "Naufragios de Álvar Núñez Cabeza de Vaca y relación de la jornada que hizo a la Florida con el adelantado Pánfilo de Narváez."

By Álvar Núñez Cabeza de Vaca. *Historiadores primitivos de Indias.* Vol. 1. Biblioteca de Autores Españoles 22. Madrid: M. Rivadeneyra, 1852. 517–48. 2 vols. 1852–53.

Weber, David J. *The Spanish Frontier in North America.* New Haven, Conn.: Yale UP, 1992.

Webster's Ninth New Collegiate Dictionary. General editor, Frederick C. Mish. Springfield, Mass.: Merriam-Webster, 1991.

Zumárraga, Juan de. "Parecer al virey [*sic*] sobre esclavos de rescate y guerra." *Don Fray Juan de Zumárraga, primer obispo y arzobispo de México.* By Joaquín García Icazbalceta. 1881. Ed. Rafael Aguayo Spencer and Antonio Castro Leal. Vol. 3. Colección de Escritores Mexicanos 43. Mexico City: Porrúa, 1947. 90–94. 4 vols.